HOUSE STYLES IN AMERICA

HOUSE STYLES IN AMERICA

THE Old-House Journal GUIDE TO
THE ARCHITECTURE OF AMERICAN HOMES

•••

James C. MASSEY and *Shirley* MAXWELL

PENGUIN
STUDIO

PENGUIN STUDIO

Published by the Penguin Group
Penguin Books USA Inc., 375 Hudson Street, New York, New York, 10014 U.S.A.
Penguin Books Ltd., 27 Wrights Lane, London W8 5TZ, England
Penguin Books Australia Ltd., Ringwood, Victoria, Australia
Penguin Books Canada Ltd., 2801 John Street, Markham, Ontario, Canada L3R 1B4
Penguin Books (N.Z.) Ltd., 182-90 Wairau Road, Auckland 10, New Zealand

Penguin Books Ltd., Registered Offices: Harmondsworth, Middlesex, England

First published by Penguin Studio, an imprint of Penguin Books USA Inc.

First printing, January 1996

10 9 8 7 6 5 4 3 2 1

Copyright © Dovetale Publishers 1996.
All rights reserved.

Library of Congress Catalog Card Number: 95-60166

Book designed by Patrick Mitchell, Claire MacMaster and Kate Gatchell
Printed and bound by Dai Nippon Printing Co., Hong Kong, Ltd.

ISBN: 0-670-86354-8

CAPTIONS FOR THE FRONTISPIECE AND PART OPENERS:

p. ii: *The sophistication of colonial Virginia's architecture is exemplified in the facade of Kenmore (1752–56) in Fredericksburg. Graced with a jerkinhead roof and a handsome pedimented entrance porch, it relies on the perfection of its proportions and craftsmanship for its effect. (Photo: Jack E. Boucher, HABS)*

pp. 4–5: *The splendor of the Georgian style is expressed in this five-part Palladian–plan house with a stately main block, richly ornamented and flanked by connecting hyphens. The wings are known as flankers. Built ca. 1783 by Major Thomas Snowden at Montpelier near Laurel, Maryland. The wings have unusual half-octagon fronts. (Photo: Jack E. Boucher, HABS)*

pp. 62–63: *The Quesset House in North Easton, Massachusetts, was built in 1854–55 in the best tradition of the picturesque Downing rural Gothic house. (Photo: Jack E. Boucher, HABS)*

pp. 106–107: *The flamboyant forms of the Victorian era are exemplified in this Queen Anne–style house, Dolobran, in Haverford, Pennsylvania, designed by Frank Furness. Built in 1881, the house was enlarged in 1894. (Photo: Jack E. Boucher, HABS)*

pp. 144–145: *One of the first of Frank Lloyd Wright's major Prairie houses is the 1902 Arthur Heurtley House in Oak Park, Illinois. This house and other early works by Wright mark the emergence of modern architecture in the United States.*

TABLE OF CONTENTS

Preface (*page ix*)

Introduction (*page 1*)

◆ ◆ ◆ ◆ ◆

◆ ◆ ◆ ◆ ◆

PREFACE

I MET JIM MASSEY and Shirley Maxwell in Washington in 1980. They were already respected elders in the preservation establishment, with credentials as historians, curators, and consultants. Jim had been Chief of the Historic American Buildings Survey (HABS), National Parks Service, and a vice president for Historic Properties of the National Trust. Yet the couple graciously agreed to have lunch with me, a youngster, to talk about writing for *Old-House Journal*, then a newsletter. Their knowledge of old buildings was neither academic nor elitist, but rather sprang from an insatiable interest in regional architecture. Jim and Shirley were in love with their work.

Shirley Maxwell and Jim Massey—partners in business and in life—apparently harbored a special fondness, even then, for OHJ's mission: to make architecture and preservation accessible to anybody who owned an old house. They even took seriously our research into early-20th-century residential architecture. It's hard to believe now, but in 1980 it was impossible to find anything written about Foursquares, Bungalows and Craftsman houses, transitional Free Classic, or even Tudor Revival houses. Jim and Shirley encouraged our foray into this uncharted architectural territory, and, over the next decade, contributed their own insights on the subject.

Of course, their writing covered a good deal more than post-Victorian houses. Their style series for *OHJ* started with the earliest houses of Massachusetts Bay and the Virginia colony, then worked its way through Georgian and Federal and Greek and Italianate. Next they turned their attention to later 19th-century styles—Second Empire, Queen Anne, Stick—educating over a hundred thousand readers and contributing to today's Victorian Revival sentiment. Along the way, this ever-spirited team dealt with vernacular structures, explained the difference between a cornice and a corbel, and made it okay to love your old house, even if it wasn't a textbook example of Style.

It seemed only reasonable to collect this delightfully accessible wisdom in one place; thus this book on American house styles. Because it covers so much more than the famous, academic examples, the book will engender some polite controversy. (Is "bungalow" a style or a house form? I say capital-B and it's a style—one so popular, in fact, that it devolved into a house form; Jim and Shirley insist it is a size-and-massing designation only.) But the important thing is that they looked at what was really built across America, not merely at the architect-designed milestones already recorded by critics. To Jim and Shirley, our appreciation and thanks.

—PATRICIA POORE
President and Editor-in-chief
Dovetale Publishers
Gloucester, Massachusetts
July 1995

ACKNOWLEDGMENTS

LIKE MOST BOOKS about architecture, this one has been a long
time in the making. In fact, it is still only a provisional conclusion
to a never-ending look at American houses: reading, writing, and
talking about them with each other and with friends and other
critics, then looking again, rethinking, rewriting. In addition to
plodding progress, there have been the usual number of wild-
goose chases, fruitful detours, and serendipitous discoveries, as
well as an occasional chastened backing out of blind alleys.
Along the way, we have found reason to be grateful to many
people, chief among them, *OHJ* editor, Gordon Bock; Dovetale's
production manager, Jim LaBelle, a valiant and capable guide
through the final passage; designer Patrick Mitchell; associate
editor Lynn Elliott; and Dovetale's resident blithe spirit, Becky
Bernie. We are grateful, too, to *OHJ*'s army of faithful readers
who have provided a stream of valuable comment, criticism,
information, and encouragement.

The Historic American Buildings Survey has provided
generous access to their superb collection of color transparencies.
We are particularly indebted to our old friend and HABS
architectural photographer-par-excellence, Jack E. Boucher, not
only for having produced several brilliant images used herein,
but also for so cheerfully unearthing them from the HABS files.

Others to whom special thanks are owed include
Susan Pearl of the Prince Georges County (Maryland)
National Capital Parks and Planning Commission; Osmund
Overby of the University of Missouri; Michael Tomlan of
Cornell University; and Jere Gibber. Whatever errors of
information or interpretation may appear in the ensuing pages
(may they be few!) will surely be fewer for the gracious
assistance of our colleagues.

INTRODUCTION

THIS IS A BOOK about American house styles. Neither a history of American residential architecture nor a compendium of America's "greatest" houses, it looks instead at broad trends in domestic building, from the first days of European settlement on this continent through the Great Depression and beyond, from saltboxes to split-levels. There are certainly mansions to be found within these pages; they help define certain styles. Yet our focus is most often not on grand houses, but on typical ones—examples that capture the essence of the everyday rather than the extraordinary (or, perhaps, the essence of the extraordinary *in* the everyday). ■ For more than ten years now, the editors of the *Old-House Journal* have encouraged us to write non-academic, unintimidating articles on the most common historic house styles for what must be one of the friendliest reading audiences in the

---

Situated in Hudson, Massachusetts, this outstanding house in the Queen Anne style was built in 1893. The seven colors that embellish the exterior make it a classic example of a Victorian Painted Lady. (Photo by Douglas Keister—Oakland, California.)

world. Like OHJ's editors, we view styles as an exceptionally friendly means of approaching architectural history—and surely the houses we actually inhabit are the friendliest way imaginable to look at styles. Eventually, there got to be forty or so such articles (including early ones by Patricia Poore) and it began to look as if they could grow up to be a book—a useful one, we hoped, since usefulness is another goal we share with OHJ. Yet this book is not a collection of reprinted OHJ articles, but a distillation of them.

Generally, the book retraces the route laid out in the articles. It begins with the first settlers' houses, which combined the skills and attitudes brought from their old homes in England, Germany, France, Holland, Sweden, and Spain with new ways and materials gleaned from the New World. It looks at the Georgian and Federal dwellings of the 18th- and early-19th centuries, followed by the first truly national style, the Greek Revival; examines the Americanization of the Gothic Revival and Italianate styles; and plunges into the "Battle of the Styles" that intensified after the Civil War, with a bewildering array of architectural choices ranging from Romanesque and Queen Anne to Stick and Shingle styles. It notes the turn-of-the-century City Beautiful movement and its interaction with Academic Classicism (Beaux Arts), early Colonial Revival, Arts & Crafts and Prairie styles; dips into Art Deco and Moderne; then moves on to International and Modern.

At OHJ's urging, we have become especially interested in 20th-century houses. Here, we have attempted to clarify major movements in the revival styles of the 1920s and 1930s: English, French, Spanish, and Colonial Revival. Our postscript touches on the "new" houses built after World War II, when revolutionary materials and construction methods sent the American house-building industry whirling toward a futuristic world of prefabs, Lustrons, ranch houses, and split-levels.

The book includes a discussion of houses best classified by form rather than style—cottages, foursquares, homestead houses, and bungalows. Although they are not always entirely style-free, such houses still manage to exist pretty much independently of architectural style, except as surface ornament. The book pays heed as well to the enormous impact of the mail-order plans and ready-cut houses that transformed American neighborhoods in the 19th and 20th centuries.

Regional styles or house types which have not influenced American residential architecture on a national scale are not generally discussed, since these vernacular forms are part of a large and complex field well beyond the scope of this volume. Shotguns, I-houses, row houses, and raised cottages, for example, are included here incidentally, as part of larger style discussions, but their many fascinating regional variations are mostly (though regretfully) omitted. Nor does the book address the important subject of Native American housing types, aside from a brief examination

1000 Forest Ave., Evanston, Illinois. Talmadge and Watson, architects, ca. 1910. A curious blend of Prairie School influences combined with traditional two-storey house shape.

of the nationally influential Pueblo Revival style. Within the limits of specific style distributions, we aimed for geographical egalitarianism, so that every corner of the nation is on display here.

All but a few photographs in the book were taken by James C. Massey over the course of several privileged decades enriched by the opportunity to study historic buildings for the Historic American Buildings Survey, the National Trust for Historic Preservation, and the *Old-House Journal*.

I. Early American Houses

Medieval
Survivors

Colonial

Georgian

Federal
& Roman

European
Influences

Medieval Survivors

[1640-1700]

T**HE FIRST EUROPEAN** settlers who came to the New World in the 17th century were understandably slow to forsake old habits. They clung, for a generation or two, to the language, clothing, customs, and architecture they had known before they set sail for America. Given the limits that life on the frontier imposed on materials, time, skills, and energy, the surviving evidence in places like New England, the Middle Atlantic, and Virginia suggests that pioneer builders did a pretty good job of recreating their European architectural heritage in America. ▪ American 17th-century houses are virtually all vernacular buildings. European vernacular house forms had changed hardly at all for several centuries before the Dutch, Swiss, Swedish, French, English, and German immigrants came to this country, and the newcomers fell back on strong ethnic building traditions dating

House of Seven Gables (Turner House), Salem, Massachusetts, was built in several stages from 1668 on. The irregular massing of additions and the massive, complex chimneys are typical of the period, and the weatherboards are typical of New England. The double-hung sash are later replacements of original casement windows.

from the Middle Ages. One major difference between building there and building here, however, lay in the choice of materials. In the 17th century, some areas of Europe already faced a lumber shortage. In America, there was more than enough wood and plenty of stone. In fact, standing timber and half-buried field stones were a hindrance to clearing the fields needed to establish prosperous farms. Happily, felled logs and prised-out rock were also the stuff of which sturdy homes could be made.

From the time of their arrival in the 1620s, English settlers in Massachusetts built a surprising number of wooden houses, given the harsh winter conditions. Masonry construction was rarely used; wooden buildings predominated, their heavy timber house frames sheathed in hand-riven weatherboards.

The steep roofs were covered in thatch at first, but the threat of fire soon convinced the settlers that wooden shingles made more sense. Massive double cross gables, on the front facade only, expanded living space on the upper storeys, while

Like most 17th-century houses, the shingled frame Coffin House (Sunset Hill) on Nantucket Island, Massachusetts, built ca. 1686, is plain to the point of severity. The name "saltbox" for this form comes from the sloping roof over a rear addition. Opposite: The Adam Thoroughgood House, Virginia Beach, Virginia, is a fine one-and-one-half-storey brick house, ca. 1640.

large, sharply sloped shed-roof additions in the rear housed service areas.

Homely Survivors

A UNIVERSAL CHARACTERISTIC OF NEW ENGLAND HOUSES was the huge, brick central chimney that warmed the whole house. Some finer examples featured big, shapely brackets and robust, turned, decorative pendants at the corners of the projecting upper storeys, both medieval practices. Even that sparse ornament was far from the rule, however, as most houses were stark indeed.

Leaded, diamond-paned casement windows, often arranged in multiples of two or three, featured a single outward-swinging section in the center with one or more fixed side sections. Single casement sash was also common, as were rectangular leaded panes. As double-hung windows with larger glass panes became available in the early 18th century, the old-fashioned casements were usually replaced, only to be restored a couple of centuries later by antiquarian enthusiasts.

The unassuming doorways of these severe houses lacked the ceremonial frontispieces that would become popular a few decades later. Heavy single doors were composed of plain vertical boards on the outside, backed by horizontal boards within.

Frame houses were somewhat less common in the Mid-Atlantic region than in New England during the 17th century. The typical early Virginia house was a small and simple affair in frame or brick, usually just one room deep and no more than one-and-one-half storeys high. End chimneys were the norm, a sensible concession to the warmer climate.

The buildings that make up the short list of 17th-century American houses still standing are a

Bacon's Castle in Surrey County, Virginia, 1665, is the finest surviving 17th-century Southern house. With its remarkable shaped gables, massive exterior chimneys, and a projecting stair tower, it is unique in American architecture. Built for Arthur Allen, it received its popular name when it was fortified during Bacon's Rebellion of 1676.

homely collection of types once common and now nearly forgotten. It may be that the most remarkable thing about them is that they have survived—altered, yet somehow changeless—to inform the appreciative observer three centuries later.

STYLE NOTES: MEDIEVAL

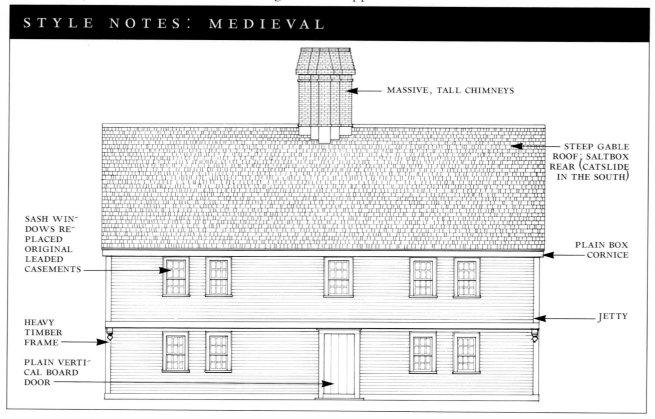

MASSIVE, TALL CHIMNEYS

STEEP GABLE ROOF; SALTBOX REAR (CATSLIDE IN THE SOUTH)

SASH WINDOWS REPLACED ORIGINAL LEADED CASEMENTS

PLAIN BOX CORNICE

JETTY

HEAVY TIMBER FRAME

PLAIN VERTICAL BOARD DOOR

COLONIAL

THE TEMPORARY DWELLINGS of the first settlers had crumbled to dust, and the sturdy timber-frame-and-brick-nogged houses of the 17th century were becoming cumbersome relics as the English colonies spread out along the Atlantic coastline in the early 18th century. Distinctive regional outlooks on building had begun to emerge, in response to New World conditions, Old World traditions—and what the neighbors were doing. ■ Early New England farmers sometimes lived in town, away from their fields, not just because of a tradition of village living in England, but also for safety and convenience. Two-and-a-half- or three-storey houses on small lots clustered cozily within the villages. Farmers also found it convenient to live close to their animals during the frigid New England winters, so many farmhouses were built to accommodate both people and cattle, although not actually under a single roof. The barn was attached by a covered access to the

The gambrel-roofed Derby House, Salem, Massachusetts, built in 1762, shows the full development of colonial architectural style: symmetry with small-paned windows and a handsome pedimented doorway.

house. In the Mid-Atlantic region, small houses and big barns were the rule. In the South, the big plantations were located far from their neighbors, but usually near rivers or other waterways that linked them to each other and to the cities.

Materials & Tradition

NEW ENGLANDERS USUALLY BUILT THEIR HOMES OF WOOD, despite an abundance of local stone. Wood was easy to work, and easier to make weathertight. So New England builders stayed with the timber-frame construction they already understood.

In the Mid-Atlantic, where good lime was readily available, there was much use of stone, as well as brick and wood. Buildings of horizontal logs were particularly quick to erect and easy to cover with the wood siding produced in the ubiquitous sawmills. The Southern colonies had plenty of clay, sand, and lime for making bricks and mortar, so brick was chosen for the most substantial dwellings. Nevertheless, buildings of wood were far more common.

Everywhere except in the lower South, there were houses with ordinary wooden fronts and backs, but brick walls at the gable ends. The brick was often set in Flemish bond, a distinctive 18th-century brick bonding pattern, and often embellished with glazed headers. In southern New Jersey and Pennsylvania, the headers might spell out the owner's initials and a construction date. A simple diamond pattern was more usual.

Northern houses, from Maine to Pennsylva-

This handsome group of colonial frame houses of the mid- and late-18th century on Union Street summarize the Nantucket house: sturdy, straightforward, and not heavily ornamented.

The Joseph Jenkins House (1773), is a large, frame house in Providence, Rhode Island's College Hill District. Its gambrel roof is especially common in New England; the twelve-over-twelve light windows and pedimented doorway typify the period.

nia, tended to be compact in their massing, making an easy-to-heat, energy-efficient package. The houses were blocky and low-slung compared to Southern examples—where houses were likely to sit over high basements or to be built on pilings. High-ceilinged rooms, favored for summer cooling, also contributed to greater overall building height in the South. Single-pile (one-room deep) and double-pile (two-rooms deep) houses with central halls allowed good cross-ventilation.

The most common roof form in all regions was the gable, often with the ridge parallel to the front of the building, but sometimes with the gable end to the front. A rule of thumb is the steeper the gable, the earlier the house, as roof pitch tended to decrease as the 18th century progressed.

A steep extension of the main roofline often covered a one-storey addition at the rear of the house creating the form called the "saltbox" in New England and "catslide" in Tidewater Virginia. Hipped roofs, sloped on all four sides, were widespread in all areas; the jerkin-head roof, with its hipped gable end, was more rarely used. Gambrels, with two different slopes on each side of the center ridge, were more common in the North than in the South. Pent eaves at the second-floor level were found mostly in the Middle Atlantic area.

Northern houses, particularly in New England and German-settled areas of the Middle Atlantic, often had huge central chimneys that absorbed heat from daytime fires and radiated it back into the houses at night. In the South, chimneys (interior or exterior) were more likely to be placed at either end of the house, letting the heat escape

---

Williamsburg, Virginia's Dr. Barraud House, built before 1796, is a common colonial house type in coastal Virginia and surrounding areas: one-and-one-half storeys with tall end chimneys and narrow dormers.

Square Tavern, Newtown Square, Pennsylvania, is a fine example of a mid-18th-century brick colonial house. Here, pent eaves between the first and second floors sheltered the lower walls against rain and snow.

outside and allowing a center-hall plan.

Plan & Features

IN NEW ENGLAND, THE FAVORED FLOOR PLAN REMAINED the "hall-and-parlor," held over from the 17th century. The first floor was divided into two rooms of unequal size, with sleeping chambers on the floor above. In this plan, the big central chimney served as many as four fireplaces. The "hall" was actually an all-purpose work and living room.

In 1684, William Penn urged German settlers in Pennsylvania to adopt a rectangular center-chimney floor plan divided into three unequal rooms: a large hall on one side, with a smaller parlor and chamber (*kammer*, or bedroom) on the other. Although it may have originated with Swedish settlers on the Delaware, the Penn plan—or, more often, a variant with outside chimneys called the Quaker plan—was used throughout the Mid-Atlantic region and upper South.

In the South, symmetrical, center-hall plans, with one room on either side of a central corridor that ran from front to rear, provided effective ventilation. The kitchen in Southern houses was often in the basement or in a separate building altogether.

The swing-out casement window with small

The 1764 Ford Mansion (also known as Washington's Headquarters) in Morristown, New Jersey, proclaimed wealth and status with a Palladian window over the door and an unusual Palladian motif for the door itself. The hipped roof adds to the stateliness. Opposite: This row of 18th-century colonial town houses in Philadelphia's Society Hill is typical of urban building practices where land was scarce and expensive. Frequently called "party-wall" houses, they share side walls for structural support, except at the end of the row.

leaded panes disappeared abruptly from both Northern and Southern houses when double-hung sliding sash came on the scene around the beginning of the 18th century. As glass became cheaper, windowpanes and windows became larger, while wood muntins grew narrower and more refined—at least until the Federal period, when the amount of wall space devoted to windows began to decrease.

Cities including Boston, New York, and Philadelphia developed their own urban forms based on the party wall. These row houses were generally two or three bays wide and as many storeys high, with the front door to one side and a long hall running back to a rear wing. Decoration was spare: perhaps an ornamental doorway and Flemish bond brickwork with glazed headers.

As the former colonies became states in a new nation, Americans' ideas about houses changed as radically as their concept of government, reshaped through an architectural response to a land in which the builders had come to feel at home.

GEORGIAN

[1740-1790]

PREOCCUPIED WITH THE business of subduing a large and not always welcoming continent, the earliest American colonists were in no hurry to embrace the latest English architectural fashions. By the 1740s, however, there was no doubt about it: the increasing wealth of the colonies was producing not merely buildings, but architecture. A bit belatedly, style had arrived in America. ▪ That first true style was what we now call "Georgian," in recognition of the era in which it flourished—during the reigns of England's first three monarchs named George, roughly from about 1700 until the American Revolution. Classical themes borrowed from the Italian Renaissance, which had been used in England, Holland, and France since the 16th century, now crept into the design of American houses from New England to Charleston and Savannah, encouraged by English

---

The stately Hampton Mansion (1783–90) in Towson, Maryland, was built by the Ridgely family in the formal, elegant Georgian style. The mansion has a commanding rooftop cupola, elaborate dormer windows, decorative urns at the roof edges, and an unusual two-storey pedimented central porch.

Drayton Hall, on the Ashley River near Charleston, South Carolina, built in 1742, is one of the finest Southern Georgian mansions, with an early two-storey pedimented porch and a double set of stone steps leading to the entrance. This large house is built on a high raised basement, typical of the Deep South.

"pattern books" containing the latest designs. The symmetrical facades and rectangular shapes of these stylish new buildings suggested the equally symmetrical floor plans that lay within, as center halls became common in affluent houses. Hipped roofs (sometimes with decks and balustrades) and lower-pitched gable roofs replaced the steep gables and gambrels of earlier colonial years. Chimneys, although still tall and imposing, were no longer the dominant features they once had been. Although American houses were rarely as large or elaborate as their English counterparts, soon a substantial number of American houses warranted the term "mansion." And decoration, once so sparingly used, took a confident turn toward the baroque.

The Palladian Plan

THE ULTIMATE EXPRESSION OF THE GEORGIAN STYLE IS the freestanding, five-part Palladian mansion. Based on the classically inspired designs of Renaissance architect Andrea Palladio, this form is composed of a sturdy main block with hyphens (a wonderfully appropriate term for these low, connecting units), which lead to smaller wings at either side (flankers or pavilions). Hyphens may be merely

Best known as the house of Henry Wadsworth Longfellow, the Craigie-Vassell House in Cambridge, Massachusetts, was built in 1759 with formal and elegant two-storey or colossal pilasters on the front and a balustrade across the top deck of the hipped roof.

covered walkways or fully enclosed parts of the building. They may extend straight out on axis or curve forward to join pavilions set at right angles to and slightly in front of the main block.

The Georgian style is sometimes described as "masculine," meaning that Georgian houses are likely to be blocky, robust, and assertive in design. The main entrance is often contained within a projecting central section, or bay, that reaches up through the full height of the house, generally two-and-a-half storeys above a raised basement.

GEORGIAN DOORWAYS WERE FRAMED WITH DECORATIVE frontispieces—showy constructions, gorgeously trimmed with lots of carved and molded woodwork. Doors might be topped by formal triangular pediments flanked by pilasters and supported by elaborate consoles or brackets—or even by that most flamboyant of Georgian door ornaments, the broken pediment, in which the arms of the triangle curve inward to frame an urn. Glazed transoms above the doors provided natural illumination to the hall. After about 1750, decorative semi-circular fanlights with thick, straight, radiating muntins came into use. The doors might be single or double, with six or eight raised panels.

In smooth ashlar stonework with stone quoins at its corners, Mount Airy near Warsaw, Virginia, was built in 1748. It is a rare complete example of the five-part Palladian plan of English country houses, with curving hyphen connectors leading from the main block to service wings known as flankers.

Not all Georgian houses were Palladian masterpieces, however. Most were virtually indistinguishable from their colonial forerunners except for their solid, broad outlines, and perhaps a handsome dentilled or modillioned cornice, a doorway graced with pilasters and pediment, and sophisticated brick and stone work. Town houses in Philadelphia, Baltimore, and Boston conserved lot space by placing gables end to end, the owners' excellent taste illustrated by heavy Georgian detail at cornices and entries.

Throughout the late 18th and 19th centuries, there was a trend toward substantial masonry buildings and more carefully finished surfaces. Georgian houses, particularly in the Mid-Atlantic, were likely to be built of stone, laid with thick mortar joints often decoratively tooled, or of brick, laid in Flemish bond with glazed headers or, later, plain headers. When frame construction was used, as it often was in New England Georgian houses,

Wye House, 1784, at Easton, on Maryland's Eastern Shore, is a condensed example of the five-part mansion.

the wood cladding sometimes imitated ashlar stonework, even down to simulated stone quoins (corner blocks) and a finish of sand laid in paint to resemble stone.

A typical Georgian window had up-to-date double-hung sash, with twelve-over-twelve panes

The conservative Quaker city of Philadelphia often built with more restraint than elsewhere, as Cliveden in Germantown, built by the Chew family in 1763, demonstrates. Nonetheless, the roof is enriched by fancy dormers with consoles and by decorative urns at the roof edges.

separated by thick muntins and a thick frame. Both frames and muntins slimmed down as the 18th century drew to a close, however, and panes increased in size as the technology for making window glass improved. Six-over-six windows were common by the beginning of the 19th century. Jib

windows, which doubled as doors that opened from the floor up to window height, were a convenience of some Georgian dwellings.

Inside, the center hall, often T- or cross-shaped for ventilation, displayed the grand central staircase that more and more often replaced

The Pierce-Nichols House, built in Salem, Massachusetts, ca. 1782 by the famed architect Samuel McIntire, is a splendid example of the robust, blocky Georgian style in New England. It is replete with monumental corner pilasters, a prominent cornice, and a balustrade designed to give the appearance of a flat roof.

Philadelphia's grandest Georgian mansion is Mount Pleasant in Fairmount Park, up the Schuylkill River from the city. Walls are of stuccoed masonry with brick quoins at the corners, and the projecting center bay features a magnificent Palladian window. The multiple webbed chimneys and rooftop balustrade add formality.

the humble corner winders of older houses. Fine woods and carvings distinguished, too, raised paneling on walls, doors, and interior window shutters. Elaborate plaster and wood trim made much of interior doorways, windows, ceilings, and fireplace surrounds and overmantels.

OF COURSE, THERE WAS NO DECISIVE YEAR—OR DECADE— when the Georgian style vanquished medieval and early colonial building customs once and for all. Instead, a floor plan was revised to accommodate a Georgian center hall; a bland colonial facade sprouted an elaborate Georgian doorway. While Georgian style still held sway, other variants of the classical forms—including the American Federal style and the Greek Revival—already nudged their way toward the front of the line.

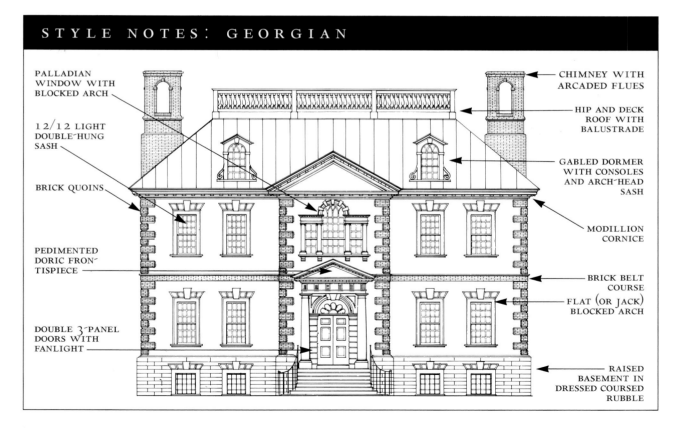

STYLE NOTES: GEORGIAN

PALLADIAN WINDOW WITH BLOCKED ARCH

12/12 LIGHT DOUBLE-HUNG SASH

BRICK QUOINS

PEDIMENTED DORIC FRONTISPIECE

DOUBLE 3-PANEL DOORS WITH FANLIGHT

CHIMNEY WITH ARCADED FLUES

HIP AND DECK ROOF WITH BALUSTRADE

GABLED DORMER WITH CONSOLES AND ARCH-HEAD SASH

MODILLION CORNICE

BRICK BELT COURSE

FLAT (OR JACK) BLOCKED ARCH

RAISED BASEMENT IN DRESSED COURSED RUBBLE

FEDERAL & ROMAN

[1790-1830]

AFTER THE AMERICAN REVOLUTION, Americans were eager to create an architecture of their own in the new Republic. Although they turned to British sources for inspiration, their ideas began to assume a distinctly American shape in the Federal style, most popular from about 1790 to 1830. ▪ The Federal style is often linked with the Georgian in architectural history because of their many overlapping characteristics. In fact, the Federal house is most easily defined by comparison with the Georgian. Its more formal and restrained outlines and details were largely in reaction to the boldness of the Georgian style. Federal lines are simpler, surfaces smoother, decoration more attenuated. Where the Georgian might have a bit of a swagger, the Federal leans toward refined understatement, frequently expressing an even more sophisticated geometry. ▪ Federal houses

Woodlawn Plantation was designed by William Thornton in 1805 at Mt. Vernon, Virginia. The traditional five-part Palladian plan, a mainstay of Georgian architecture, continued into the Federal period in a simpler, more restrained form.

*The Gardner-Pingree House is a classic Federal-
style mansion: a large, three-storey brick box,
restrained but elegant in design. Built in 1804–5,
probably to a design by Samuel McIntire, it is part of
the Essex Institute in Salem, Massachusetts.*

often include curving or multisided bays, elliptical rooms, semi-circular or octagonal bays or porticoes, domed and arched ceilings. They are more
likely than the Georgian to be three full storeys
high or, conversely, much more likely to have only
a large single storey above a raised basement. The
five-part form seen in the Georgian was also used
for Federal mansions, even for one-storey buildings.

FEDERAL DOORWAYS DISPLAYED FAR LESS WOOD THAN THEIR
Georgian counterparts; columns and pilasters were
slim and light. They often had semi-circular fanlights, but elliptical fans with delicate tracery in
wood or lead are a distinctive Federal feature.
Muntins were thin, flat, and delicate, even when
they were ornamental. Sidelights and, where there
is no curved fanlight, transoms are also frequently
seen in Federal buildings. Six- or eight-panel, sin-
gle- or double-leaf doors were common. Federal
houses often featured double- or triple-sash windows that extended to the floor.

Federal ornament is smaller and infinitely

*The crowning glory of Federal-era Salem,
Massachusetts, is Chestnut Street, lined with elegant, late-18th- and early-19th-century mansions.*

quieter than Georgian, inspired by the work of Robert Adam, who had developed a refined interpretation of decorative motifs from classical antiquity. Under his influence, the noisy splendor of Georgian woodworking was gradually muted and replaced by the subtler rhythms of the new century. Where heavy masonry string courses wrapped around blunt Georgian facades, the plain surfaces of Federal buildings were likely to be broken only by shallow recessed or applied panels. Where virtuoso Georgian woodcarving might once have dominated a pediment, Federal swags and cartouches now discreetly insinuated themselves.

Jeffersonian

THE "MOST ROMAN OF THE ROMANISTS," THOMAS Jefferson gave a personal twist to Federal architecture. Jeffersonian Classicism, or Roman Revival, was far from Adamesque or Greek. Jefferson considered the Roman arch and dome not only more beautiful than Greek post-and-lintel construction or English Georgian design, but also

Tudor Place (1794–1816), by William Thornton, shows the Federal-style transformation of the Georgian Palladian plan. It overlooks the historic Georgetown district of Washington, D.C. The Federal period saw wide use of stucco to create a more finished wall surface than brick alone; tripartite windows; and low roof lines. Tudor Place has an unusual semi-circular half-domed portico, echoed within the house. This use of non-rectangular shapes is a feature of the period.

better suited to the building needs of the new world, from homes to banks and city halls. Roman buildings also symbolized the republican ideals of the American political experiment.

Jefferson's two Virginia homes, Monticello and Poplar Forest, illustrate his architectural tenets. The designs for dozens of other buildings throughout the United States before 1830 are attributed to his hand—or to his advice. The University of Virginia, known to this day as "Mr. Jefferson's University," is among his most notable contributions to public architecture.

Jeffersonian buildings exhibit simplicity, symmetry, restrained but emphatic classical ornament, and dignity. Exquisite proportions count more than decoration: spare Tuscan columns, for instance, rather than Corinthian. Jefferson's years in Europe and his careful reading of Andrea Palladio, 16th-century classicist, are manifest in five-part house

The 1804 Read House faces the Delaware River in New Castle, Delaware, serenely demonstrating the transition from Georgian massing to the self-possessed restraint of Federal detailing. The entrance with arched transom and narrow sidelights is a common Federal feature. The delicate, curved wrought iron of the second-floor Palladian window railing is also characteristic of the period.

plans with central blocks and flanking wings, important porticoes (both front and rear), polygonal shapes, and temple forms.

Among others who designed houses in the Roman style are James Hoban and William Thornton (architects of the White House and Tudor Place, respectively). Jefferson's influence on American architecture was broad, deep, and long-lived. With those of other Federal architects, his concepts provided an apt and beautiful basis for the architecture of the emerging republic and a strong link between a colonial past and a nationalist future.

Monticello, Thomas Jefferson's residence and masterpiece near Charlottesville, Virginia, was built in many stages and remodelings from 1770 to 1808. It reflects Jefferson's interpretation of a functional house: finely scaled, in one storey above an English basement, separating servants' areas from those to be served.

EUROPEAN INFLUENCES
[1690-1860]

THE BRITISH WERE NOT the only early settlers who brought ideas about house building to America. Immigrants from Germany, France, Spain, Holland, Sweden, and other European countries also contributed ethnic traditions. Distinctive traits hung on well into the 19th century, sometimes reappearing with later groups of newcomers. They help account for the regional differences that charm and fascinate old-house enthusiasts. ▪ French and German building practices spread throughout the eastern half of North America, following settlement patterns. German houses that look a lot like their prototypes along the Rhine River can be found in Pennsylvania, Maryland, and Virginia, and also in former Moravian religious settlements from New Jersey and Pennsylvania to North Carolina and the Virgin Islands. In the mid-19th century, a new wave of German immigrants to Texas, Wisconsin, and Missouri built new houses based on the building traditions of

This small, mid-18th-century Germanic log house on a stone foundation is the Kleiser Log House in York County, Pennsylvania. Note the pent eaves all around; many German and English houses once had them.

home. Settlers from France, or from French colonies in the West Indies and Canada, built their own vernacular style around the Gulf of Mexico from Florida to Louisiana and along the Mississippi River north to Missouri and Illinois.

THE EARLIEST GERMAN BUILDINGS IN THIS COUNTRY were usually made of rubble stone or heavy tim-

ber framing filled in, or "nogged," with bricks. This half-timber construction, known as *fachwerk*, made the most of two common building materials. In the old country, buildings were nogged because timber for building was in short supply; in America, the timber framework helped compensate for the shortage of lime needed for strong mortar and hard bricks. *Fachwerk* was quickly replaced by brick or frame construction in the East, but reappeared in German-settled areas of the Midwest. There it may be filled with stone, brick, or straw and clay.

A typical example of German influence in early American building is the single-storey cabin with an central chimney and stove designed to serve both the kitchen and the *stube*, or parlor. In stone buildings, segmentally arched window and door lintels relieved much of the stress of the heavy building material. Doors typically were constructed of diagonal boards. "Kick" roofs with a slight flare near the edge are supported by ceiling joists that extend through the exterior walls. Often the Germans built above freshwater springs. In Missouri and Wisconsin, a few traditional German housebarns can still be found, where family and farm animals

Fort Zeller, perhaps the most Germanic of all the early houses, built in 1745 in Newmanstown, Pennsylvania. Opposite: A half-timbered house, in La Grange, Texas, in the midst of the Texas hill country. This area was settled in the 1840s by Germans who brought with them their traditional half-timbered fachwerk construction.

EUROPEAN INFLUENCES

51

Immigrants from Holland settled in the area around New York City, including Long Island, along the Hudson River, in northern New Jersey, and New Castle, Delaware. The John Taylor House (Marlpit Hall), ca. 1700, Middleton, New Jersey, is a typical Dutch frame house displaying the characteristic steep shingled roof with an outward kick at the bottom and shingled walls. Opposite: The Pommer House, 1839–40, home of a prosperous German settler in Herman, Missouri, is closer to Federal style than traditional German, but with typical continental double doors ornamented with Germanic paneling.

shared the same roof, if not the same living space.

It's generally believed that the Swedes built the first horizontal log structures in America. But lush forests offered a ready supply of the raw material, and other European settlers, including the Germans, began building them. The log house soon became common in the Northeast; of course, as settlement moved westward, it became the house type remembered as a symbol of the frontier.

French Traditions

FRENCH HOUSE-BUILDING IN THE NEW WORLD WAS VERY different. While French settlers knew how to build with horizontally laid logs (a process they

called *pièce-sur-pièce*), early French houses in America were often built of vertical posts sunk into the ground *poteaux-en-terre* fashion—literally, "posts in the ground." A few survive in Missouri.

Other houses, also often short-lived, were built *poteaux-sur-solle*, with their posts mortised into a sill resting on the ground. *Poteaux-en-terre* and *poteaux-sur-solle* are more closely related to half-timbering (which the French called *colombage*) than to horizontal-log construction, since the spaces between the upright posts are nogged with bricks, or *bousillage*, a mixture of clay and dried moss. Wooden braces helped hold the nogging in place, and wood siding or an exterior plaster coat were additional protection. Still, the structures were very vulnerable to water damage.

The French solved the problem of rotting foun-

The Krebs House ("old Spanish Fort"), a fine early 18th-century French Gulf Coast house with surrounding gallery and steep hipped roof, in Pascagoula, Mississippi.

dations and melting nogging with the one-storey raised cottage, the hallmark of French-influenced architecture in the Gulf Coast states. Built by immigrants from the French West Indies who had experience with heat and torrential rain, these houses stood on piers that allowed air to flow freely beneath the buildings. Steep, double-pitched, hipped roofs sent rainwater cascading downward, and deep porches kept it safely away from walls and windows.

The flared roof and the *galerie*, or encircling porch, of French Colonial dwellings in the Mississippi Valley arrived by very different routes. But they've been seen together so often that they now seem like one phenomenon. The steep, central portion of the roof, or *pavilion*, was brought by French colonists from Quebec, where it had dispatched rain from thatched roofs. The *galerie* was brought to America by the West Indian French.

Like other vernacular designs from the colonial period, those of French settlers incorporated elements of the Georgian, Federal, and Greek Revival styles as they came along. Center-hall floor plans and symmetrical facades, hipped roofs and double-hung sashes—they all slipped easily into the old vernacular, creating by the 1830s an unmistakable Creole style.

Spanish Architecture

THE SPANISH SETTLEMENTS IN THE UNITED STATES WERE not concentrated in a few areas but were spread, often sparsely, across the nation from Puerto Rico and Florida to the Southwest and the California coast. Each area of settlement, far-flung over 300 years and thousands of miles, developed its own idiom. Perhaps the most consistent tradition developed 800 miles offshore, in the Caribbean Island commonwealth of Puerto Rico. Spanish influence there

Pitot House in Bayou St. John, 1779, in what was then a rural suburb of New Orleans, with a two-storey gallery that became common on Louisiana plantation houses.

Monterey, California's Larkin House, started in 1835, is the best example of the Monterey style, with two-storey galleries and a low-hipped roof. Opposite: An arcaded patio with louvered shutters against the heat of the sun from a private house in Old San Juan, Puerto Rico.

was strong and direct.

In the Southwest, ancient stone and adobe pueblos dovetailed with the Spanish emphasis on masonry walls and indigenous building materials. Later, Eastern Anglos contributed the Greek Revival details that resulted in New Mexico's Territorial style and California's Monterey style.

Churrigueresque ornament, a baroque style of decoration named after 16th-century architect José Benito Churriguera, was much admired and sometimes appeared in New Spain's most grandiose churches, as did more restrained classical motifs. But such ornament is unheard-of in domestic buildings.

What most distinguishes this architecture is a layout that turns toward a central court for safety, privacy, and a sense of the outdoors. Plans featured courtyards and small *placitas* formed by long lines of rooms on two or more sides. Old San Juan has the best examples. Entire towns, in fact, were a single file of end-to-end houses wrapped tightly around central plazas that served as marketplaces, civic centers, and social venues.

Just as characteristic are the arcades, or *por-*

tales (long, narrow, roofed-over rows or arches and columns), that created sheltered walking and sitting areas outside, evoking the cloistered walks of mona-steries. Front porches later came into fashion. In the Southwest, these were supported by rough, round timber posts decorated with carved and painted brackets at the roof. Multiple exterior doors were common. Early doors are low and constructed of plain plank, turning on pintles rather than hinges. Only a few doors of this period are carved and paneled.

Windows were few in the thick masonry walls, especially early on. Window reveals, deeply splayed to maximize light, rarely contained glass, but were protected instead by iron bars or shutters. By the 1830s, windows were larger and more likely to be glazed and have wooden framing, sometimes alluding to the Greek Revival or Italianate fashion. Stuccoed masonry of one sort or another was generally the rule for walls. Rooflines might be gabled and gently sloped (as in California), hipped (popular along the Gulf Coast and the Mississippi), or flat and possibly parapeted (especially in the arid Southwest). Flat roofs actually had an almost inperceptible slope and a system of *canales* (interior drains) to carry runoff away from the vulnerable wall. A series of *vigas* (round timber beams)

The famed Palace of the Governors in Santa Fe, New Mexico, was started in 1610, with the portal added in 1705. It exhibits typical features of adobe construction and was restored in 1909.

was a safe and familiar support system. On top of the *vigas*, the roof was built up with several layers of mud plaster and small sticks—and covered with tiles, when cost was not an obstacle.

ALONG THE GULF OF MEXICO AND THE MISSISSIPPI RIVER, where control shifted from one European power to another, we find the celebrated blend of Spanish, French, and English influences, the French flavor predominant.

Masonry contruction may have been the rule, but material and style differed widely. In Florida, houses were built of *coquina* (a soft local stone composed of shells and coral) or *tabby* (a limestone and oyster-shell aggregate). Builders in the Southwest favored blocks of *adobe* bedded in a mud mortar and covered with mud-plaster finish. The Pueblo Indians were already accustomed to *adobe*, which they laid in long strips; the Spanish innovation was to mold it with wood forms into manageable blocks.

Of particular note in the Southwest are the tiled roofs so dear to the 20th-century Spanish Colonial Revival. In the 18th century, they were recognized as a fireproof alternative to thatch.

IN TEXAS AND ARIZONA STAND THE MOST SOPHISTICATED of the Spanish Colonial buildings, those most faithful to the styles that flourished in Spain during the period. San Antonio was within relatively easy travel of Mexico City, an advantage that resulted

in several outstanding churches and missions. One is the Alamo, which had an honorable career as a mission before it became the ruinous fort.

New Mexico's *adobe* pueblos, missions, and churches show far more Indian than Spanish influence. After the American Civil War, however, the Territorial Style—a late blossoming of the Greek Revival with a distinctive New Mexican twist—became the state's popular building mode. It announces itself not only in wood trim, but also in the narrow line of brick corbeling at roof parapets and in brick trim around windows and doors.

California is noted for its extant string of 18th-

Typical of the early houses in St. Augustine, Florida, is the 1720 Arrivas House that has a coquina first storey with frame second level. Opposite: Mission San Gabriel Archangel (1812), in San Gabriel, California, is one of the famous chain of Pacific Coast Spanish missions.

century Spanish missions snaking up the Pacific coast from Mexico to just north of San Francisco. During the Victorian era, the porches and balconies of Monterey Style houses were decorated with sawn-wood balusters like those of 19th-century porches across the country. In California, too, we find *haciendas*, the original ranch houses.

II. Romantic Houses

Greek Revival

Gothic
Revival

The Italian
Styles

Exotic
Revivals

GREEK REVIVAL

[1820-1860]

IN THE FIRST HALF of the 19th century, Americans leapt head, heart, and hand into a long, passionate attachment to all things Greek. The democratic ideals of Greece were then being reasserted in the Greek War of Independence from the Turks, recalling the American Revolution. The beauty of classical art, literature, and architecture shone brightly in the light of archeological discoveries of the period. Greece's civilizing role in the ancient world was a model for America's dreams for its own future. ▪ Not surprisingly, then, Greece provided the inspiration for the predominant building style used in the many new houses and towns built between 1830 and 1860. Most of these buildings were not intended to replicate ancient structures, but to adapt them for use in America's new "National Style" or, as later generations would rename it, the Greek Revival style. ▪ For much of the mid-19th century, the Greek Revival style dominated construction

Houses like this typical Greek temple-front house in Bristol, Rhode Island, can be found in numerous locations from Maine to Illinois. It has a full pedimented Ionic order portico front, and a typical door with transom and sidelights—a design of unusual appeal.

One of the grandest and most "correct" temple-style mansions in the United States is Andalusia, built near Philadelphia for Nicholas Biddle. In 1835, architect Thomas U. Walter designed this handsome portico with a Doric colonnade around three sides.

in every state east of the Mississippi River, as well as in those bordering the western banks of the Mississippi, with occasional scattered examples in other western states. The ready availability of American pattern books, the new access to trained architects, the widespread system of transportation improvements (roads, canals, railroads), and the need to house the great migratory waves that surged out of the northeastern and southern United States, as well as directly from Europe, all contributed to this style that was not only nationwide, but nation-making as well.

The major regional distinction was between North and South: The full-height columns extending across the entire facade of a building, which have come to epitomize the ante-bellum Southern

The simple Greek Revival Walkup House in Crystal Springs, Illinois, lacks the temple portico, but has the gable front, deep fascia, and door with transom and sidelights that signify the era. This particular example is a cobblestone house, so-called for its wall construction of natural rounded stones found in a geological belt from Vermont west to Wisconsin and northern Illinois.

mansion, are found less frequently above the Mason-Dixon Line, while front-gabled, corner-pilastered flat facades are less often seen below it.

The Greek Orders

THE MODEL FOR GREEK REVIVAL ARCHITECTURE WAS THE ancient Greek temple, in which a series of columns supported a horizontal superstructure called an entablature, or a triangular pediment. In the United States, the style was based, rather loosely, on the Greek "orders": sets of building elements determined mainly by the type of column that was used. The columns ranged from the simple Doric, with a fluted shaft and cushion-shaped capital, through the Ionic, with a capital shaped like an inverted double scroll, to the elaborate Corinthian, whose foliate capital might be carved in any plantlike form. The Tuscan column, a simpler, Roman version of the Doric, had no fluting on the shaft.

In the Greek tradition, there was always an

The Levi Starbuck House (1838), in Nantucket, Massachusetts, is a high-style Greek Revival house without a full-height portico. Its main facade, with a small but elegant Ionic entrance porch, looks into a side garden. The pedimented gable end facing the street also has deep, attached, two-storey pilasters.

A more nearly perfect example of an Ionic order Greek-temple house portico would be hard to find. This is the Judge Robert S. Weber House in Ann Arbor, Michigan, ca. 1839.

even number of columns (generally four or six), in order to avoid a center column. Americans felt free to use five when it suited their purposes. The columns could be placed in front of the building only (prostyle) or all around it (peristyle). They could be beefed up with antae (square columns also called piers or pilasters) at the sides of the building, or with engaged pilasters almost anywhere. If there were two columns in the middle with piers at the corners, the building might be described as *distyle in antis* (two columns between posts). Frequently, a bit of architectural sleight-of-hand implied the presence of columns where there were none, with ranks of shallow wooden pilasters set almost flush with the wall surface.

The pediment was also a versatile and economical device for vernacular use. Turn a boxy, gable-roofed Georgian or Federal house with its narrow end to the front, add a heavy horizontal band from corner to corner, and there's your "pediment." Even the band could be omitted, for deep "returns" at the lower angles of the gable gave the illusion of a full triangle.

Defining Details

BRICK AND, FOR IMPORTANT BUILDINGS, STONE, PREFERABLY ashlar, were popular building materials, but wood was also frequently used. According to contemporary accounts, most wooden buildings were painted stark white with green shutters. Faux finishes were commonly used to simulate more

expensive materials, and flush wooden siding or brick walls were frequently stuccoed and scored to resemble stone.

It is rare indeed to find a Greek Revival house without an impressive doorway. Multipaned transoms, sidelights, paired columns, and pilaster trim created an impact in the simplest entryways. Doors were either single or double, with anywhere from one to six panels. Greek Revival windows were often floor-length, or nearly so, with six-over-six or nine-over-nine panes and thin muntins in double- or even triple-hung sash, or with jib doors. Wooden panels sometimes filled any space between the bottom of the window and the floor. Almost a cliché of the period are frieze windows, small horizontal windows set in a row under the cornice and often covered by a decorative wooden or iron grille.

Ornament was always bold, in deliberate contrast to the Federal period. Greek Revival ornament was easy to produce using modern tools, and the development of rail and water transportation made it easy to get the ornament to frontier areas. This was also the era in which it became possible to produce cast ironwork, and fine cast-iron window grilles, roof crestings, and porch railings were widely used.

IT WAS ONLY AFTER THE CIVIL WAR THAT PICTURESQUE and revival styles of other times and places, particularly the Gothic Revival, finally loosened Greek Revival's grip on the American imagination. Prob-

Chicago's famed "Widow Clarke House," now rescued and restored, is best called the Henry B. Clarke house, built in 1836. The Doric portico extends across the middle of the house only; one did not need a full temple front to be stylishly Greek. The square cupola with rounded windows appears more Italianate and is probably a later addition.

ably the most enduring legacy of the Greek Revival style is the gable-front house, the standard form of the 19th century farmhouse. Until well into the 20th century, the gable-front was also one of the dominant forms for detached city houses in the Midwest and Northeast.

Greek Revival forms and ornament reached far down into the vernacular level to touch farm-houses and workman's cottages of the mid-to late-19th century. The tiniest, one-room-wide shotgun house often boasted a couple of flat pilasters, a columned doorway, or a row of Greek ornament across its narrow front. The forward-facing gable, with or without ornament, was the distinguishing mark of the era's most popular house type, the two-storey Homestead, or temple-form house, which sprang up on farms and in urban rows across the nation.

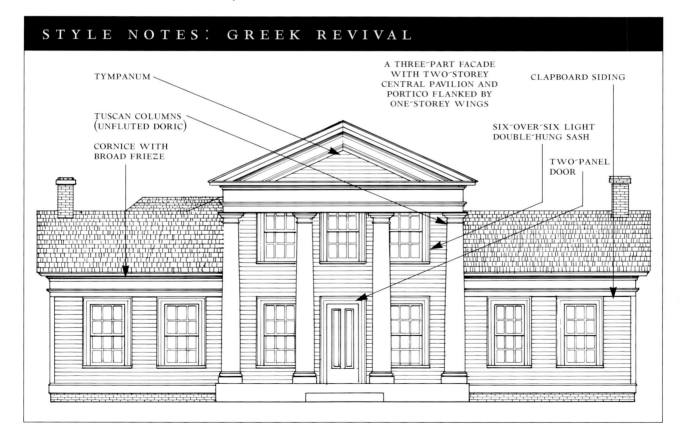

STYLE NOTES: GREEK REVIVAL

TYMPANUM

A THREE-PART FACADE WITH TWO-STOREY CENTRAL PAVILION AND PORTICO FLANKED BY ONE-STOREY WINGS

CLAPBOARD SIDING

TUSCAN COLUMNS (UNFLUTED DORIC)

SIX-OVER-SIX LIGHT DOUBLE-HUNG SASH

CORNICE WITH BROAD FRIEZE

TWO-PANEL DOOR

GOTHIC REVIVAL
[1830-1875]

W HAT A GRAB BAG OF STYLES confronted—and sometimes confounded—the discriminating 19th-century American house-builder! From the neoclassical to the exotic, there seemed no end of architectural choices in this restless era. Greek Revival, Gothic Revival, Egyptian, Moorish, and Italianate all had their champions in what has been aptly described as the "Battle of the Styles." Although no rival ever outshone the century's hands-down favorite building style, the Greek Revival, there were two serious challengers to the boxlike symmetry of classical architecture. The Gothic Revival and the Italianate styles both appealed enormously to the romantic mood of the era with their picturesque, asymmetrical massing and ornamental variety. ■ America's distinctive approach to Gothic evolved

The Hermitage, Ho-Ho-Kus, New Jersey, started out as an 18th-century Dutch house constructed of local stone in a rich, reddish brown. A fine Gothic remodeling and addition (1847-8, William Ranlett, architect) provided a striking gable pendant boss, flamboyant ornament on the bargeboards, and clustered porch columns. The gable roof sports fish-scale wooden shingles and angled chimney stacks. The Gothic Revival period marked the first widespread use of sitting and service porches.

Lyndhurst, designed in 1838 by A.J. Davis and enlarged by him in 1860, is the greatest of the Gothic castles in America. It sits high above the Hudson River in Tarrytown, New York, and was once a fitting home for railroad magnate Jay Gould.

over many decades. In the 18th century, medieval decorative motifs were simply pasted onto Georgian or Federal-style buildings. The 1830s brought serious imitations of English rural parish-church architecture of the Middle Ages, using irregular shapes and plans. At the same time, a rural Gothic style was developing, based loosely on the English country cottage of the same period, and popularized by architectural pattern books aimed at the middle-class homebuilder, especially A. J. Downing's *Cottage Residences* of 1842. In this book and others, architects Andrew Jackson Downing and Alexander Jackson Davis preached the benefits of healthful country living in attractive new Gothic "cottages" or villas. Like all Gothicists, Downing stressed that buildings should express their functions, materials, and construction "truthfully." Honest houses, for instance, had porches and large chimneys to show that people lived in them, and frame buildings would never be painted to imitate stone.

The fact that the buildings they copied were most frequently constructed of masonry, usually stone, perturbed American builders not a whit. They were perfectly content to use good old abundant American wood for simple cottages

and to leave the stone and brick for grander structures. Although clapboard or flush siding was common, vertical board-and-batten construction came closer to the desired vertical effect while still honestly expressing humble building materials and construction techniques. Most home-builders had no need in their light, balloon-framed, wooden houses for flying buttresses, vaulted arches, and the other structural inventions that enabled 13th-century stonemasons to build soaring churches. But they liked using Gothic ornament very much indeed.

With its triple front gables reaching steeply to the sky, and its marvelously decorated bargeboards, the John Bibb House in Frankfort, Kentucky, is one of the nation's most memorable Gothic Revival houses. Note that it is brick, perhaps the least-used material for Gothic Revival houses. Opposite: The first important West Coast Gothic rural cottage in the Downing mode is Moss Cottage, in Oakland, California, built 1864 by S.H. Williams, architect, with an unusual projecting center front gable bay over the entrance porch.

Newport, Rhode Island: Kingscote, designed by Richard Upjohn and built in 1839–41, one of the earliest Gothic "cottages" in the ultimate summer resort of Newport. Here flat "matched" flush siding in wood gives the impression of cut ashlar stonework.

Two main types of Gothic houses emerged. The pointed (or rural) Gothic featured very steep gables, ornate bargeboards, and abundant use of the pointed, or lancet, arch. On the other hand, battlements, parapets, and square towers dominate the castellated, or castlelike, Gothic. The pointed Gothic form, whether cottage or mansion, was found most often in rural settings, and may look out of place in a crowded urban site. The castellated Gothic was better suited for city living and for large country mansions.

Motifs

THE MOST PREVALENT "GOTHIC" FEATURE IN HOUSES was the very steeply pitched gable roof, often trimmed with a wooden scrollwork bargeboard (or vergeboard) pierced with such Gothic motifs as trefoils, quatrefoils, cusping, or rows of pendant pointed arches. Instead of the standard double-hung windows, casements were frequently used, often with diamond-paned glass. Small, one-storey entrance porches with fanciful trim; large, striking chimney pots; clustered columns with chamfered edges; Tudor arches—all were icing on the Gothic-Revival cake.

Elaborate cast-iron ornament, such as rooftop

*Wesleyan Grove, an 1860s summer camp meeting
ground on Martha's Vineyard, Massachusetts, features
streets of these fanciful, small Gothic cottages.*

cresting, was a hallmark of especially stylish Gothic homes. In rural areas, heavy, carved stone bargeboards were replaced by wooden scroll-work produced by a new machine, the scroll saw, in the thoroughly American folk style now called Carpenter Gothic. This self-consciously rural style often featured the board-and-batten siding recommended by Downing and Davis.

The Gothic Revival style spread rapidly throughout the United States, all the way to California and Oregon. It was not as widely used in the Deep South as in the northeastern and mid-western states. Although the Gothic Revival lingered until nearly the turn of the century, its longevity manifested in forms ranging from cottages to churches to skyscrapers, it eventually faded in the face of the pre–Civil War enthusiasm for the Italianate style.

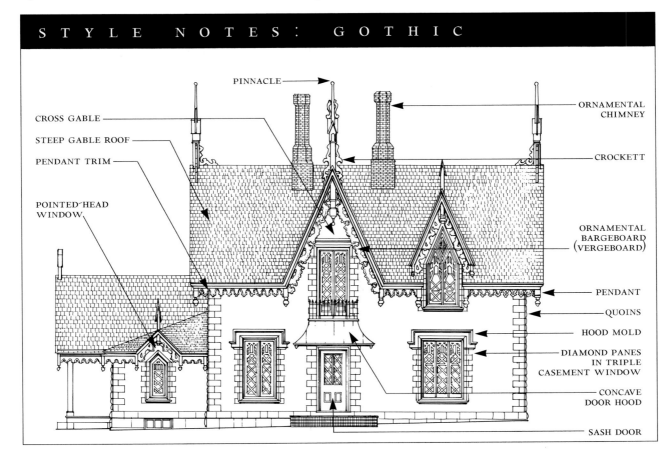

STYLE NOTES: GOTHIC

- PINNACLE
- CROSS GABLE
- STEEP GABLE ROOF
- PENDANT TRIM
- POINTED-HEAD WINDOW
- ORNAMENTAL CHIMNEY
- CROCKETT
- ORNAMENTAL BARGEBOARD (VERGEBOARD)
- PENDANT
- QUOINS
- HOOD MOLD
- DIAMOND PANES IN TRIPLE CASEMENT WINDOW
- CONCAVE DOOR HOOD
- SASH DOOR

GOTHIC REVIVAL

THE ITALIAN STYLES
[1840-1890]

THE AMERICAN CIVIL WAR was preceded, by a decade or so, by a different sort of strife within the world of architecture. The new Italian style was gaining ascendancy over the Gothic Revival and challenging the enormously popular Greek Revival. By the 1860s, it was the most fashionable architectural style in America. ■ Italian-style houses fall into three basic categories: Villa, Renaissance Revival, and Italianate. Villas were intended to evoke the farmhouses and manors of the Italian countryside. The term included both the asymmetrical Italian Villa, with its prominent tower, and the Tuscan Villa, a square building with deep, bracketed eaves. The Italian Villa's irregular shape allowed architects to ignore the demands of symmetry and focus on convenience, with floor plans designed to allow people to move easily throughout the house. In addition to asymmetry,

The Governor Henry Lippitt House, in Providence, Rhode Island, by Henry Childs, builder, has a magnificent rounded entrance porch in the most stylish Italian manner. Here the formality of mid-19th-century interpretations of the Italian Renaissance is dominant over the picturesque, and more popular, Italianate villas.

The Andrew F. Scott House, with its cupola, wide eaves, projecting front bay, and verandah, was built in 1858 at the high point of the picturesque Italianate house. Located in the major railroad-junction town of Richmond, Indiana, it shows the rapid spread of the style into the Midwest.

the telltale signs of the Italian Villa include a low-pitched roof and deeply overhanging eaves supported by heavy, decorative brackets. Sometimes these houses have a center gable, relatively low-pitched, with overhanging eaves. But the Italian Villa's defining feature, according to 19th-century architect Andrew Jackson Downing and his circle of Romantics, was its square entrance tower, or *campanile*, ideally placed somewhat off-center to enhance the building's asymmetrical charm. The tower was usually tucked into the angle of an L-shaped plan and extended a storey or so above the rest of the house.

The much simpler Tuscan Villa was built far more frequently. Like Italian Villas, Tuscan Villas have heavily bracketed cornices. What distinguishes the Tuscan style is its extremely symmetrical box shape and flat roof, often with a *belvedere* centered on top, as shown at left.

Urban Renaissance

THE RENAISSANCE REVIVAL STYLE WAS BASED ON THE FORMAL, highly symmetrical palaces, or *palazzos*, built during the Renaissance in Tuscany and northern Italy. It was used for mansions as well as town houses, and can be recognized by its formal, sym-

The houses of New Orleans, Louisiana, are always distinctive, as this Italianate with the traditional fancy New Orleans cast-iron balcony demonstrates. This is the Andrew Johnston House of 1879 by William Fitzner.

A typical I-house in Virginia's Shenandoah Valley, the Myer House at Mount Olive, was built in the 1870s around an earlier small cabin. The I-house form—three-bay front, one room deep, often with a rear wing—was built throughout the South and Midwest in the mid- to late-19th century. The gable over the center bay is common. Stylistically, these houses are Italianate. As is often the case, the porch was probably a later addition.

metrical shape and heavy cornice.

Renaissance Revival was a favorite style for city row houses of this era. These town houses feature a heavy, bracketed cornice and a stair or stoop to the *piano nobile,* or main (second), floor. The basement level of Renaissance Revival row houses is usually rusticated. Quoins, or heavy corner blocks, are another prominent form of exterior ornament. Entrance doors are heavily hooded, and there are often keystoned arches above the windows.

In its purest form, the Renaissance Revival palazzo was used more often for public buildings than for houses, but several noted architects did produce some handsome mansions in the style. True palazzos were always built of masonry, either stone or stuccoed brick. Quoins typically set off

Philadelphia's Woodland Terrace, designed by Samuel Sloan in 1862, is the finest surviving street of picturesque Italian Villas, replete with wide eaves, porches, and offset towers.

the main building sections. Ornament is more restrained and classical than in the Italian Villa. Renaissance Revival eaves, for instance, are more likely to display sedate dentils and modillions rather than big, showy, paired brackets.

The Italianate

ITALIANATE HOUSES, THE MORE VERNACULAR AND BY FAR the most common examples of the Italian style in America, are neither villas nor palazzos, but they do include many of the architectural details found on their more pretentious cousins. Becoming popular after the Villa styles were already well established, the Italianate style persisted until the late 1880s.

The overwhelming majority of these houses were not high style or custom-designed. All a builder had to do was flip to an Italian-inspired plan in one of the many pattern books published during the period. Even more often, builders started with a familiar-shaped house and simply added a few of the very fashionable Italianate details.

Italianate houses were made of any available material, from brownstone to brick to wood. Often, though, the materials were used in a way that would mimic the stone of their Italian Villa and palazzo models. Exterior surfaces were usually flat, often stuccoed, sometimes "pencilled" or scored to resemble masonry blocks, and painted in muted,

stonelike colors.

As a rule, Italianate windows were large, using double-hung sash set one-over-one. Bay windows and oriels were common; so were windows with round-arch tops. Windows were almost always shielded by flat-topped, rounded, or pediment-shaped hoods; or they were framed with wide, flat, scrolled trim.

Porches were a nearly universal feature of

The Norton House, 1849–50, by Henry Austin in New Haven, Connecticut, exemplifies the Italian Villa at its most picturesque: irregular massing, ever-present tower, wide eaves, and arcaded porch. Austin was a master of the style, meant to recall rural Italy.

the Italianate house, especially small entrance porches. Larger one-storey porches, called verandahs or piazzas, became popular as the century pro-

The Hay House in Macon, Georgia, built in 1860 by architect T. Thomas, represents the most formal phase of the Italian style, more directly derived from Renaissance prototypes than were the picturesque Italian villas.

The 1850s Whimsey House, in Topsfield, Massachu-setts, reminds us that not all Italian-style houses have low roofs with cupolas and towers. Many gable-roofed houses belong to the Italian style. Note the broad eaves with paired brackets and the handsome quoins imitating stone at the corners of this frame house.

gressed. The porch was always a major focal point of the facade. It often led to double front doors with round tops and molded trim; round-arched door panels produced a similar effect. Porch supports,

most often square or with chamfered edges, appear frequently in pairs. Bracketed tops rather than column capitals are also distinctive to the style.

After reigning for several decades, the Italian styles finally began to ebb in the 1880s, a victim of circumstance. During the 1870s, post–Civil War economic troubles curtailed home construction. By the time housebuilding resumed in force, a new repertoire of architectural styles—Romanesque, Queen Anne, Shingle and Stick-style, Colonial Revival—had captured the American imagination.

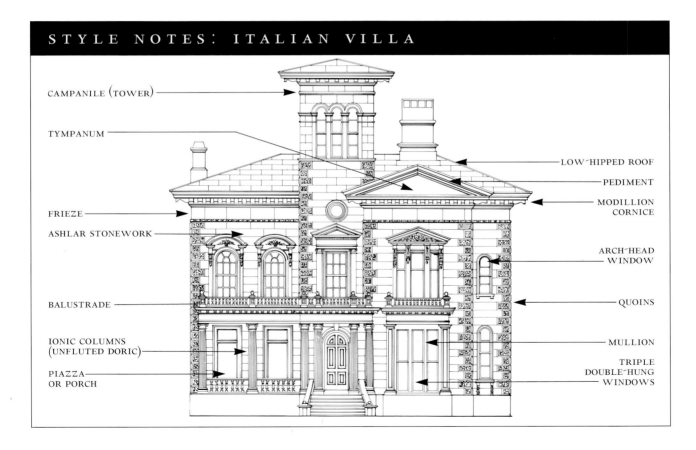

STYLE NOTES: ITALIAN VILLA

CAMPANILE (TOWER)

TYMPANUM

FRIEZE

ASHLAR STONEWORK

BALUSTRADE

IONIC COLUMNS
(UNFLUTED DORIC)

PIAZZA
OR PORCH

LOW-HIPPED ROOF

PEDIMENT

MODILLION
CORNICE

ARCH-HEAD
WINDOW

QUOINS

MULLION

TRIPLE
DOUBLE-HUNG
WINDOWS

EXOTIC REVIVALS

[1840-1880]

I**N THE LONG LIST** of American house styles, a few leave an impression bigger than the number of built examples warrant. Two 19th-century imports from the Middle East—the Egyptian Revival and the Moorish Revival—come to mind, along with the intriguing shapes of octagonal and round houses. ▪ The architectural forms of Egypt captured the imagination of Europeans and Americans alike. Sphinxes, pyramids, obelisks, and temples hinted at age-old secrets suddenly made accessible to the Western world. Egyptian-style cavetto moldings, winged orbs above windows and doors and on cornices, papyrus and palm columns, pylons, and hieroglyphic markings were symbols of ancient wisdom. ▪ Rational to the core, 18th- and early-19th-century intellectuals found the

Egyptian Revival, the most exotic of all 19th-century revivals of the ancient past, was a bit too exotic for houses, but it suited jails and cemeteries just right. This is the Moyamensing Prison Debtors Wing in Philadelphia, Pennsylvania (T. U. Walter, 1836), built in an age when you could be locked up for not paying your bills—thus making it a residence, if not exactly a house. The facade features motifs from ancient Egypt. The cavetto (cove) cornice, winged disc, and battered (sloping) walls were the most common features.

rect buildings, only the exterior appearance of the structure was affected. When it came to interiors, Eastern architectural precedents were ignored. The heavy stone foundations of authentic Egyptian buildings used up a lot of precious floor space; most Egyptian-Revival buildings looked bulkier on the outside than they actually were on the inside.

THE MOORISH REVIVAL STYLE, WITH ITS FAT, ONION-SHAPED domes and cusped arches, is only a little better represented than the Egyptian Revival in American houses. When it does appear, however, it is likely to be as exhilarating as the Egyptian is sobering.

In the United States, much of what we think of as Moorish-Revival architecture evolved by way of Muslim influences on Spanish architecture during the Moorish occupation of that country from the 8th through the 15th centuries. Happily, two remarkable Moorish houses survive here,

geometric discipline and hard edges of Egyptian forms very appealing. In practice, though, these forms showed up mostly as decorative elements added to buildings designed in whatever popular style prevailed at the time. A few battered columns or pylons attached to the face of a cubical or rectangular (often Italianate) building were enough to establish the desired relationship. Even in the more archaeologically cor-

both now historic house museums. The most exotic is Longwood (also known as Nutt's Folly) near Natchez, Mississippi. Longwood was designed by the Philadelphia architect Samuel Sloan for Dr. Haller Nutt, a well-educated "scientific" farmer. Begun in 1859, it was inspired by a design for an "Oriental Villa" that was published in Sloan's *Model Architect* (1852–53). Although its interior plan is fairly symmetrical, the exterior shape of Longwood is an irregular octagon—an Italianate villa rendered picturesque by the addition of Moorish-Revival ornament.

Olana, near Hudson, New York, was the much-loved 250-acre estate of the renowned Hudson River landscape painter Frederic E. Church. Unlike Longwood, Olana is no symmetrical Italian villa overlaid with bays and galleries, but a truly picturesque mansion. In collaboration with the architects Frederick Clarke Withers and Calvert Vaux, Church managed to achieve a much purer Moorish form—although one that even the happy owner described as "personal Persian"—using irregular massing and strong Moorish references such as arches and polychrome tiles.

No other major 19th-century Moorish Revival houses remain. Although circus mogul P.T. Barnum built himself a Moorish mansion, Iranistan, in 1848, it was demolished. Like the Egyptian Revival, the style is seen mostly in details and ornament, including tile work, arches, and domes.

Breaking the Square

IN THIS PERIOD IT WASN'T ONLY EXOTIC ORNAMENTAL motifs that were explored. Some American builders wondered why we build our houses as squares and rectangles when circles, octagons, and other offbeat shapes offer so many more opportunities. Circles and octagons contain more interior space per square foot of wall area, for instance, so they (theoretically) cost less to build and heat. They make it possible to place windows to take full advantage of sunlight or breezes from any direction.

This miniature octagon fantasy is in the garden of a real three-storey 1854 octagon, the John Richards House in Watertown, Wisconsin. Opposite: A model of the type of octagon house promoted by Orson Squire Fowler in his popular book of 1848, A Home for All: *the 1850s Glebe House in Arlington, Virginia, replete with a splendid porch and cupola, topped by an immense wooden eagle.*

The best-known proponent of octagonal houses was Orson Squire Fowler, a noted phrenologist, who propounded what he considered a perfect building form, the octagon, and a promising new material, an aggregate cement invented by Joseph Goodrich of Milton, Wisconsin. Fowler promoted octagonal houses in his 1848 *A Home for All*, which attracted wide popular interest.

The doctrine of the octagon was particularly well received in Michigan, Ohio, Wisconsin, Massachusetts, and New York (Fowler's home state), where hundreds of octagons were constructed. In fact, with all the public praise heaped

From its start in New York, the octagon fad spread across the nation. This one, handsomely painted in Victorian colors in Barrington, Illinois, is from the 1850s. Opposite: The rarest of house forms is the circle, which enjoyed a brief flurry of interest. The best surviving example is the Enoch Robinson House in Somerville, Massachusetts, built ca. 1852.

upon octagonal and circular buildings, it seems that they might have become one of the most common house types of the 19th century. Not so. Most medium-sized towns from the period had one—and probably only one—octagon, a comment upon

Opposite: The best-known octagon is the Armour-Stiner House at Irvington, New York, built in 1860 by a New York financier. The impressive dome and cupola were added in 1872. (Photo by Douglas Keister–Oakland, California.) Below: This 1873 hexagonal house in Winchester, Virginia, is perhaps even less convenient in interior arrangements. Stylistically, it is Italianate.

both the emotional appeal and the practical limitations of the form. For the truth is that while the octagon has many advantages, it also presents certain rather sticky problems. A lot of leftover, odd-shaped corners and triangles result when traditional rectangular rooms are inserted into the octagonal plan. So, while hundreds of octagonal houses were built, thousands more were merely dreamed of over a well-worn copy of a Fowler book.

The octagon is an architectural form, not a style; it has always accommodated whatever frills and furbelows the builder's taste demanded. Fowler himself was not particular about stylistic details, but most owners of octagonal homes in the 19th century chose Italianate or Gothic ornament.

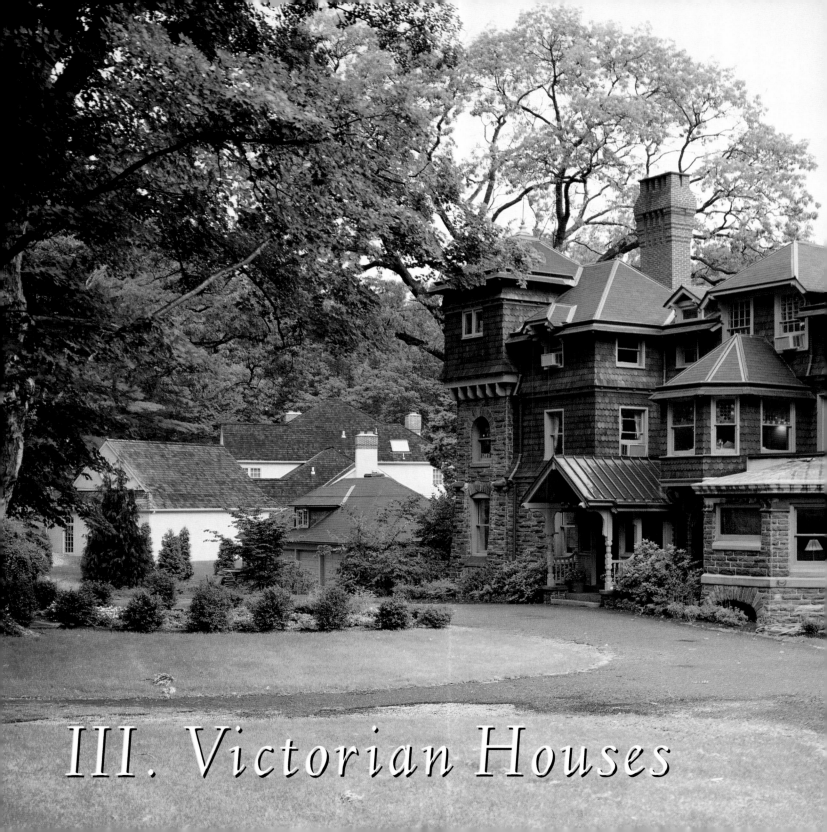

III. Victorian Houses

Second
Empire

Romanesque
Revival

Queen Anne

Stick &
Shingle Styles

Mail-Order
Designs

SECOND EMPIRE

[1855-1885]

I**F THERE'S A STYLE** that shouts "Victorian!" to the 20th-century house enthusiast, it must be Second Empire. Actually, Mansard Style would have been a better name for Second Empire in America. It is the distinctive, double-pitched mansard roofline that settles the question of whether a house belongs to this French-inspired genre. No matter whether the house is I-shaped, four towering storeys high, or a single storey plus an attic: if the roof is a mansard, the house will be called Second Empire. ▪ Between about 1855 and 1885, this new style from France, named in honor of the era in which Napoleon III and Empress Eugénie reigned, was enthusiastically adopted in this country. It was embraced more widely in cities (where the mansard roof was a stylish way of adding an extra storey to a row house) than in rural areas, and more in the Northeast and Midwest

The Hubbell House, Terrace Hill, is now the Governor's Mansion in Des Moines, Iowa, and one of the nation's finest Second Empire houses. Of lively design, bold decoration, and an unusually tall tower, it has the characteristic mansard roof that defines the style and provides it with its alternative name, the Mansard Style. Terrace Hill was built 1867–1869 by the prominent Chicago architect William Boyington.

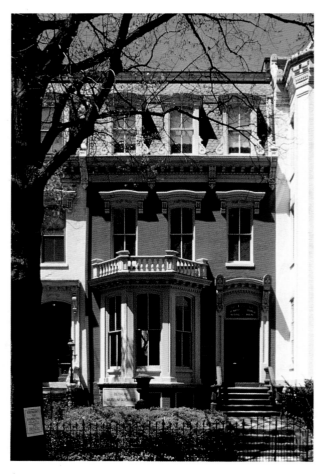

The Mary McLeod Bethune House, ca. 1872, a National Historic Landmark in Washington, D.C., is a typical urban party-wall house of the post–Civil War period. Opposite: Indianapolis's Morris-Butler House of 1859–62 has a fine concave mansard roof and a four-storey tower. The arched windows and entrance, porch, and side bay window are typical of the period.

(where the major cities were) than in the South and West.

Named for the 17th-century French architect François Mansart, the mansard roof consists of a very steep lower slope and a gently angled, almost flat top portion. A boxy, straight-line mansard roof was most common, but the trendiest thing in Second Empire rooflines was the curve—bulging outward (convex), scooping inward (concave), or looping about in a giant S (ogee-shaped). Large houses with towers and wings often combined several roof shapes; only porches were exempt (usually) from the mansard craze.

Slate was the preferred building material for this type of roof. Tin and wood shingles were also popular, but not just any shingle. Fashion dictated that the shingles had to be multicolored, fancifully shaped, and laid in intricate patterns. Large dormer windows almost always pierced the roofs to light the extra storey. Ornate cast-iron cresting marched along the roof ridge or around a central deck, and towers were likely to be topped by cast-iron pinnacles or finials. Tall, elaborate, brick chimneys completed the impressive Second Empire roofline.

The style may have been based on French Renaissance architecture, but it was seen in this country as a very modern style, not a historical throwback as were the Gothic and Greek Revivals. So builders, never pedantic about constructing "pure" examples of a particular house style, felt even freer to take liberties with Second Empire.

"Heavy" is a useful adjective for Second Empire: heavy stone or brick wall surfaces (or wood

imitating stone); heavy ornate trim, and lots of it, at windows and doorways. Holding it all down was The Roof. The look was solid and self-assertive, sometimes downright overbearing.

The vast majority of mansard houses were decorated in whatever the current styles and the owners' whims suggested, in whatever quantities their pocketbooks could handle. Since this was the era of machine-turned wooden and pressed or cast-metal trim, there was usually a good bit of it. Italianate ornament was by far the favorite choice. However, other decorative styles were also present in pro-

The Queen Victoria Inn, in Cape May, New Jersey, built in 1881, is resplendent in Victorian colors. Note its full-height corner bay windows, projecting center bay, and verandah across the front.

fusion. The Stick Style, for instance, is quite evident in vernacular Second Empire houses.

Second Empire houses are usually at least two or three storeys high, sometimes four, not counting the attic storey. Outside the big cities are found mansard cottages, with only a single storey below the mansard. While masonry, most often brick, was the preferred building material for mansions, most mansard-roofed houses were of light, balloon-frame construction with wooden siding. The weighty look was achieved through the judicious use of dark, stonelike paint colors. Occasionally, corners were finished with counterfeit stone quoins made of wood, but usually they were covered by simple vertical boards painted in even darker shades. These corner treatments served to make the house look sturdier, and to draw the eye upward to—what else?—the Roof.

Porches invariably played a prominent role in late-19th-century domestic architecture. Porches were often tacked onto these houses with what looks like reckless abandon. The most fashionable porches were small, one-storey, somewhat boxy affairs. (This was not an era that favored round shapes.) The porch posts were usually, but not always, square and paneled. On less pretentious houses, the porch was very often a full-width, honest-to-goodness "sitting porch."

Windows were often grouped in pairs or threes. They were generally Italianate: round-topped, square-headed, or pedimented, capped by hood moulds, surrounded by moulded or scrolled panels. Small round (oculus) windows were often tucked in wherever they would fit, and sometimes

In Red Hook, New York, a convex mansard on the tower stands in attractive contrast to the main roof's concave mansard, all embellished by decorative iron cresting on the rooftops.

little rectangular "monitor" windows paraded across the frieze beneath the cornice, recalling the Greek Revival. Ample windows set in bays and oriels let in still more light. Wood trim was often painted with pigment mixed with sand to make it look like stone. Sash was usually painted a dark color.

Where does the Italian style leave off and the

Second Empire begin, and when did the style fall out of fashion? The Second Empire came into vogue at an unusually eclectic period in American architecture, a time when new ideas lurked behind every pilaster and there was a rich mix of ornamental influences. It's safe to call any 19th-century building with a mansard roof "Second Empire." But to see what else is going on, remove (mentally, please) the roof and take a look at what's left. It could be Italian, Greek Revival (or even Federal), Romanesque, Queen Anne, or Shingle Style.

Following the end of Napoleon III's reign in

Opposite: Boston's Back Bay was built up after the Civil War with predominantly mansard-roofed, party-wall houses, such as this 1872 house at the corner of Clarendon and Marlborough Streets.

1870 and the financial wars of the mid-'70s, the Second Empire fell out of favor almost as quickly as it had reached its peak. The style did linger in some areas, but most architectural mentions of Second Empire were in articles telling homeowners how to update their musty old mansards into lively Queen Annes.

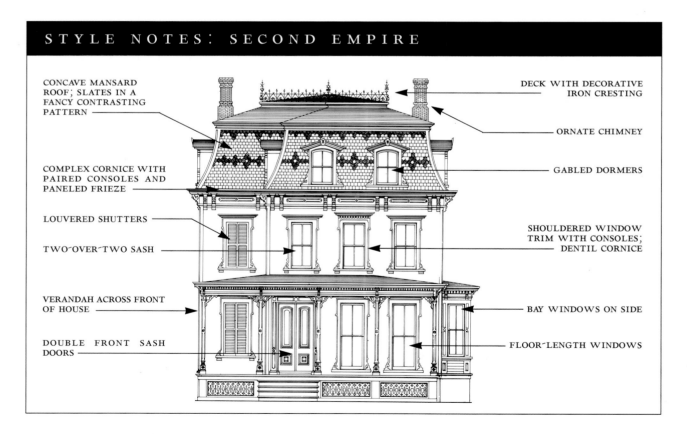

STYLE NOTES: SECOND EMPIRE

CONCAVE MANSARD ROOF; SLATES IN A FANCY CONTRASTING PATTERN

COMPLEX CORNICE WITH PAIRED CONSOLES AND PANELED FRIEZE

LOUVERED SHUTTERS

TWO-OVER-TWO SASH

VERANDAH ACROSS FRONT OF HOUSE

DOUBLE FRONT SASH DOORS

DECK WITH DECORATIVE IRON CRESTING

ORNATE CHIMNEY

GABLED DORMERS

SHOULDERED WINDOW TRIM WITH CONSOLES; DENTIL CORNICE

BAY WINDOWS ON SIDE

FLOOR-LENGTH WINDOWS

ROMANESQUE REVIVAL
[1870-1900]

T HE ROMANESQUE REVIVAL—popularly called Richardsonian Romanesque—is such a formal style that you would hardly expect it to turn up in ordinary houses. Yet how else to explain all those city brownstones with shadowy entrances set back deep behind low-slung arches embellished with terra-cotta jungle growth? What of the dark masonry fronts on block after city block of late-19th-century row houses? Romanesque's reign was short—as a residential style, it first appeared in the 1870s, hit its stride in the late '80s, peaked in the '90s, and was virtually gone by 1900—but its impact on the faces of our Victorian cities was deep and lasting. ▪ Much like the Gothic Revival, the Romanesque Revival began in the 1840s and 1850s as a historical revival of medieval European and English church architecture, and it was used primarily for churches and pub-

The Conrad House on St. James Court in Louisville, Kentucky: A fine stylish Romanesque stone house with a corner tower and the ubiquitous, rounded-arch entrance porch on squat, thick colonnettes. The house was designed by Clark and Loomis and built 1893–95 at the end of the Romanesque period, as people started to clamor for the quite different Colonial Revival style.

lic buildings. Richardsonian Romanesque, on the other hand, was a truly American style, adapting Romanesque forms and decorative motifs in innovative ways. Architects began to use the style for houses in the 1870s.

Henry Hobson Richardson, the young architect who domesticated the Romanesque style and brought it into the American vocabulary, was no slave to history. His interpretation of the medieval Romanesque was so fresh and powerful that in the United States the style became inseparably linked to his name. His talent catapulted Romanesque Revival to architectural stardom. Ironically, its widest popularity came after his untimely death in 1886 at the age of 47.

This was not a poor man's style. The Romanesque was a reflection of what many well-to-do Americans felt about themselves at the end of the 19th century: substantial, prosperous, and very sure of their places in the world. A man's home was his castle—his fortress, in fact—and the Romanesque Revival was the style to drive that point across. Thick, impenetrable walls; corner-tower lookouts; turrets and tall, half-round bays. These

edifices lacked only a moat and drawbridge.

The building material of choice was masonry, preferably ashlar (square-cut) stones, generally with rough or "rock-faced" surfaces set in broken-range (uneven) patterns. Brick and terra-cotta also made a strong impression at lower cost. Because

the technology for applying veneer layers of stone or brick as a facing had yet to be developed, walls were solid in reality as well as in appearance. To provide variety in texture and color, architects commonly specified two or more kinds and hues of stone. Brownstone (the popular term for a reddish-brown sandstone) was used so frequently that its name became synonymous with the town houses of this era. It was a soft stone that could readily be carved into the intricate shapes late Victorians loved. They were especially fond of half-formed, viney foliage that seemed to be heaving itself bodily out of the rocky surfaces of lintels and column capitals.

Main rooflines were often gabled, sometimes very steeply gabled, although on row houses they tended to be flat. Towers and turrets wore conical "witches' hats." Slate was the preferred roofing material. Corbeling (projecting rows of brick-

work) along the eaves replaced the brackets of the Italianate and Second Empire styles.

Windows in a Romanesque building were most likely to have round-arch heads or, failing that, straight, heavy lintels, usually of rock-faced stone. The windows were deeply recessed, often grouped in sets of two or three and unified by a common stone lintel or a linked row of arches. By this time, one-over-one-light windows, with a single pane of glass in each sash, were universal in "modern" buildings such as these. Often a rectangular tran-

In South Bend, Indiana, the Studebaker Mansion of ca. 1890, by Henry Ives Cobb, has a corner entrance porch with rounded arches, multiple colonnettes, and unusual, irregular stonework for its walls.

som ran in a band across a set of square-headed windows. Arcades (rows of arched openings, windows, or doors) were a feature of the style. Usually three or four storeys tall, buildings often had dormers to light the upper level.

Romanesque doorways sank even deeper into

The interior courtyard and garden at the Glessner House in Chicago, one of H.H. Richardson's masterworks, reveals a warm and picturesque private space in the city, contrasting with the severe design of the street facade.

wall surfaces than did windows, protected from ill winds and prying eyes behind heavy stone arches. Porches sometimes became internal affairs, tucked under the second floor as part of the ubiquitous recessed entry. The porte-cochère (covered carriage entrance) was an important feature of many freestanding houses of this era; chances are that it, too, would have had its own impressive arch.

The use of arcades was not confined to window and door openings. In earlier Romanesque Revival buildings, "blind" arcades (recessed slightly into, but not through, the wall surface) took the place of eave brackets, even marching up the sides of the "A" on gable-roofed buildings.

All those arches required some form of support, of course, and it usually came from columns or piers. The columns might be grouped in pairs or in clusters of colonnettes; they might be tall or short, stout or slim, plain or decorated. The most popular were short, stout, and decorated. The low, wide, Syrian-style arch that came into use at this time was virtually all arch and no column.

The Richardsonian Romanesque was intended for large, grand, freestanding buildings. When this style reached the popular level—in party-

ROMANESQUE REVIVAL

123

wall town houses, for example—it was inclined to lose some of its dash and dignity. Houses based on vaguely Richardsonian and Romanesque ideas were often a hodge-podge: a tower here, an arch there, a bit of figurative ornament on a column or a lintel, all appearing on standard spec-house plans to produce a picturesque effect. Finding round corner towers unworkable in continuous rows, local builders were more likely to substitute flattened-out bays or oriels. There was no reason to forego arched windows and entryways, however, and Romanesque ornament was too tempting to pass

A typical Romanesque "witch's hat" in copper caps the tower of the Heurich Mansion in Washington, D.C., designed by John G. Myers, 1892–94.

up. Such elements stood in for the whole style.

The Romanesque style possessed all the faults inherent in its virtues. In uninspired hands, its weightiness came across as just plain gloomy. Its claims to dignity might have seemed pretentious; its formality felt stiff. Other popular styles, namely the Queen Anne and Shingle, were lighter baggage to carry in the journey toward a new century.

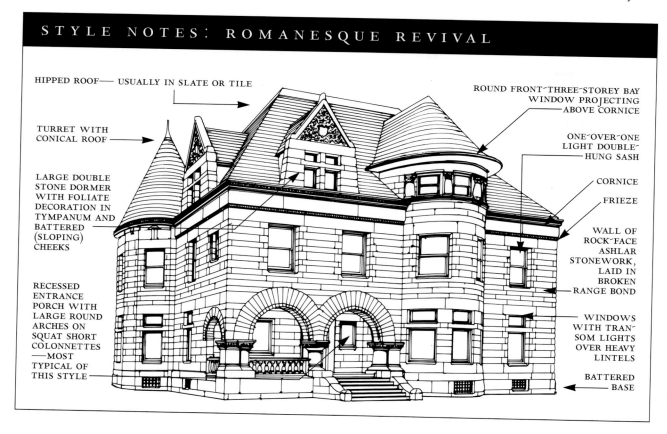

STYLE NOTES: ROMANESQUE REVIVAL

HIPPED ROOF—— USUALLY IN SLATE OR TILE

TURRET WITH CONICAL ROOF

LARGE DOUBLE STONE DORMER WITH FOLIATE DECORATION IN TYMPANUM AND BATTERED (SLOPING) CHEEKS

RECESSED ENTRANCE PORCH WITH LARGE ROUND ARCHES ON SQUAT SHORT COLONNETTES —MOST TYPICAL OF THIS STYLE

ROUND FRONT-THREE-STOREY BAY WINDOW PROJECTING ABOVE CORNICE

ONE-OVER-ONE LIGHT DOUBLE-HUNG SASH

CORNICE

FRIEZE

WALL OF ROCK-FACE ASHLAR STONEWORK, LAID IN BROKEN RANGE BOND

WINDOWS WITH TRANSOM LIGHTS OVER HEAVY LINTELS

BATTERED BASE

QUEEN ANNE

[1870-1910]

F OR MOST OF THE 19th century, American architects were obsessed with the idea of finding a truly American style. They looked everywhere for it—in ancient Greece, in the Italian countryside, in medieval churches, and even in the Middle East. Each of these tacks seemed promising ... but they were not really American. ▪ Then, in the 1870s, American designers came upon the work of Richard Norman Shaw, an English architect specializing in a style that presumably represented building during the early-18th-century reign of Queen Anne. Actually, the half-timbered cottages that Shaw and his American admirers liked so much were a bit earlier than Queen Anne (say, by a hundred years), but nobody minded. A Queen Anne style was just the thing—and something really American was about to happen to it. ▪ Spurred on by architectural books, the style then took off

Hale House, ca. 1887, now in Heritage Square, Los Angeles, is attributed to the best known of California's Victorian architects, Samuel and Joseph Cather Newson. It features their typical, overly elaborate and robust Eastlake decoration.

across America. In one form or another, its popularity stretched from the late 1870s through the first decade of the 20th century. And why not? This style had something for everyone, and builders in Queen Anne would do almost anything to provide visual treats. The new Queen Anne cottages were as picturesque as their Gothic cousins, but less "gloomy" and with no suggestion of a religious origin. They emphasized vertical lines with plenty of steep gables, and they had very few boring, flat wall surfaces. There were angles everyplace, alternately catching and absorbing light. Towers and bays projected,

verandahs and niches receded, chimneys surged skyward. Up, down, and across the building, the walls were fairly alive with changes in materials—brick,

In Springfield, Missouri, the Bentley House, 1892, is a mature Queen Anne example with restrained forms, but retaining the corner turret, ample verandah, porte-cochère, and half-timbering in the gables. Opposite: The Watts-Sherman House in Newport, Rhode Island, designed by Henry Hobson Richardson in 1874, is the first great example of the American Queen Anne style.

In Los Angeles, the Mooers House of 1894 has the robust, exotic abandon of Eastlake ornament— heavy, elaborate, and partial to curves. Note the porch, the gables, the fancy turned work, and the sweeping curved ornament within the entrance pediment to the verandah. Opposite: In Bay City, Michigan, this large and handsome house illustrates the common practice of drawing from several styles in a single building. It displays something of the Queen Anne style in the small-paned windows and modillion cornice; Eastlake in the vigor of its ornament; Stick Style in the structural expression and panels of its frame walls.

stone, stucco, shingles, tiles, wood siding, clear and stained glass—and color. This was American.

The style could be adapted to houses large enough for the biggest family. But unlike the massive Romanesque, it always seemed welcoming and respectful of human scale. It worked in the city on narrow lots, and in the country on farms and estates. It worked in wood or masonry, with or without half-timbering. Floor plans could be individualized almost endlessly, with porches and verandahs and towers and bays added at will.

Style Variants

THE FARTHER THE STYLE TRAVELED FROM ITS SOURCE, the more likely it was to change. It became simpler as it was used in vernacular buildings. Less affluent owners might not be able to afford stained-glass

windows or slate roofs or tall, fancy chimneys, but they probably could manage a bit of wood spindlework. A 19th-century American ornament, spindlework was a product of our love affair with the newly invented turning lathe, which, along with an efficient railway system, made it cheap and easy to decorate houses all over the country, inside and out, with rows and rows of shapely little sticks. Today, such spindlework may furnish the only clue to the Queen Anne aspirations of an otherwise plain, gable-fronted house.

Whenever the site and the budget allowed, there were sitting porches and verandahs, the lat-

With ample verandahs, a forward projecting gable, and Old English half-timbering, these double, or twin, houses on Philadelphia's Main Line in Wayne, Pennsylvania, are a splendid pair of Queen Anne houses. Opposite: In Jackson, Tennessee, the Wisdom House is a classic example of the American Queen Anne: a mixture of Old English decoration, informal massing, and Victorian design.

ter intended for promenades in inclement weather, but also useful as outdoor extensions of the parlor. The style lent itself to sheltered entrance porches, recessed balconies, and other niches and projections. Also, there were specialized porches for a variety of household service functions: washing clothes, preparing foods and so on.

Windows were an eclectic mix and important to the style's vocabulary. Besides the swinging case-

ments with small, diamond-shaped panes (reminders of medieval inspiration), there were other more practical (and more common) kinds. Stained, leaded, and etched glass was common, but few Victorian homeowners could ignore the benefits of huge, machine-made panels of clear glass that had become readily available. Consequently, colored glass is often confined to transoms or to borders of small panes placed around the edges of a large upper panel of clear glass set in a standard one-over-one, double-hung sash.

Color was an essential element in Queen Anne design. No glaring white for these houses; and if the owners had an ounce of good taste, no mud colors either. Professional advisors suggested that small houses be treated to light, warm, neutral colors, while larger houses could handle darker neutrals, with trim in a darker shade of the wall color. Brick and shingles should not be painted, owners were warned, but shingles might be dipped in paint the color of red tile. Green was acceptable for exterior blinds (shutters) if a harmonizing color such as Indian red were used as a buffer between the shutters and the neutral wall color. On recessed features, such as inset doorways and balconies, there was no need to avoid "positive" colors. Picture Henry Hudson Holly's recommendation for a recessed doorway: "The exterior walls should be buff; the sides of the enclosure, a deep ultra-marine green, trimmed in Indian red with lines of black; the coved ceiling, a

Reliance, Virginia: A rambling, rural village Queen Anne with an ample verandah and a small tower that is almost Italianate. Opposite: New Orleans, Louisiana: Deep in the Garden District is this stylish frame Queen Anne with an overhanging second floor on the side, characterstic sash windows, a handsome front bay window, and a small recessed entry porch.

brilliant blue." (Fortunately, paint manufacturers by this time were able to provide fairly accurate color chips and mostly consistent colors, no doubt, preventing a world of colorful disasters.)

In city houses, particularly in the East, where there were fewer opportunities to create irregular wall surfaces and where fire codes required greater use of masonry walls, contrasting colors of brick, stone, and tiles were used to produce similar poly-

chromatic effects. Prominent chimneys added interest to the building. The westward migration of professionally trained architects brought incredible elaborations in later Queen Anne-style houses in California and other parts of the far West, as well as in the Deep South.

In much of the country, the preferred roofing material was slate. Wood shingles, tin, and, on more expensive buildings, copper were also used. The important thing was to have not just one roof, but several, peaked or hipped or both. How many sleepless rainy nights do Queen Anne owners endure as

This sturdy small Queen Anne in West Chester, Pennsylvania, lacks some of the elaborate detail that marks much of the style, but includes such basic features as an ample front verandah, a corner octagonal bay and turret, and a decorative chimney.

sacrifice on the Altar of the Picturesque, when those hips and valleys begin to leak?

Ah, but the sacrifice is joyfully made. Because in the course of its long and varied lifetime, didn't this misnamed architectural hybrid become, after all, a really American style?

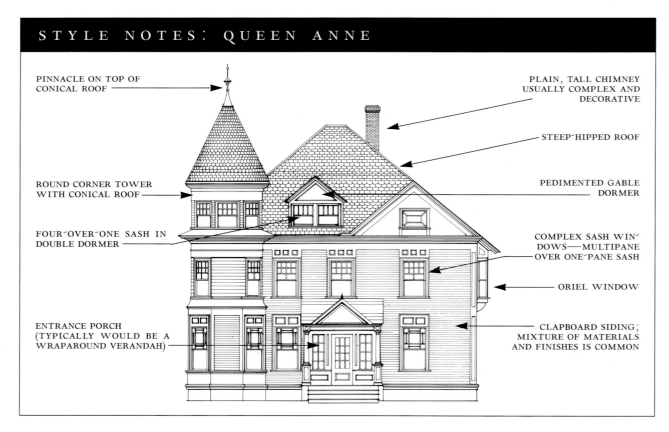

STYLE NOTES: QUEEN ANNE

PINNACLE ON TOP OF CONICAL ROOF

ROUND CORNER TOWER WITH CONICAL ROOF

FOUR-OVER-ONE SASH IN DOUBLE DORMER

ENTRANCE PORCH (TYPICALLY WOULD BE A WRAPAROUND VERANDAH)

PLAIN, TALL CHIMNEY USUALLY COMPLEX AND DECORATIVE

STEEP-HIPPED ROOF

PEDIMENTED GABLE DORMER

COMPLEX SASH WINDOWS—MULTIPANE OVER ONE-PANE SASH

ORIEL WINDOW

CLAPBOARD SIDING; MIXTURE OF MATERIALS AND FINISHES IS COMMON

STICK & SHINGLE STYLES

[1870 - 1905]

THE CONTRASTS BETWEEN the Shingle Style and the slightly earlier Stick Style show the tensions being worked out in American architecture during the last three decades of the 19th century. Both Shingle and Stick were quintessentially American styles meant to be built in wood, but the material was handled very differently in the two cases. Whereas the Shingle Style concentrated on what might be called the skin of the building, the Stick Style emphasized its bones—that is, the cross braces and vertical and horizontal wood framing on the exterior walls were intended to "express" the internal construction of the building. While the framing sometimes looks a bit like half-timbering, it was actually the more modern balloon-framing technique that was meant to be expressed since these wooden pieces were generally only superficial decoration. The characteristic, stick-like brackets, however, provided real support for high-pitched gable roofs with deep eaves.

This Gloucester, Massachusetts, house exhibits the charm of the Shingle Style in a rocky seaside setting, with ample wraparound verandahs and picturesque Old English timbering with stucco in the gables.

The Physick House in the Victorian seaside resort of Cape May, New Jersey, designed by Frank Furness in 1878, exemplifies the Stick Style, with horizontal siding making panels decorative rather than structural. With walls such as these and the use of struts for the eaves and porch, the house looks as if it were made from sticks.

Other distinguishing features include irregular building shapes and deep verandahs.

The basic Stick Style orientation was vertical, an offshoot perhaps of the High Victorian Gothic, with a touch of Swiss chalet. Yet, with all its peculiarities, the Stick Style, like the Shingle, was moving toward a more modern, more distinctively American approach to building design.

One look at a Shingle Style house and it's easy to guess how the style came by its name. This 1880s seaside-resort fashion is wrapped from its rooftop to its stone foundation—or, at the very least, to its masonry ground floor—in what seems to be a continuous sheet of dark wood shingles. Not all shingled houses are Shingle Style, of course, but nobody is likely to confuse these large-scaled houses with the small, vernacular wooden dwellings of colonial New England that inspired them. The term itself wasn't used until the mid-20th century, so late-Victorian builders were more likely to refer to their new constructions simply as "cottages with shingles." Like the Queen Anne and Romanesque styles, the Shingle Style blossomed through the '80s and '90s. It was never as popular as the Queen

Detroit's Charles Long Freer House, 1887, by the noted Philadelphia architect Wilson Eyre, exhibits the smooth overall shingle mass that typifies this style, here on top of a stone first-floor base. Typically, the design is informal and picturesque, suggesting its place in the larger Arts & Crafts movement. Opposite: In Morristown, New Jersey, a Stick Style house, less exuberant and more restrained than some, giving it a homelike character.

Anne, however, and it faded away in the early years of the 20th century, although not without leaving its mark on houses to this very day.

Shingle Style houses were first built in New England as summer homes—mansion-sized "cottages"—for the wealthy. They spread to other areas of the country as well, from Midwestern suburbs to California, where some of the most delightful examples are found. Shingle Style houses made poor candidates for city dwellings. Their sprawling habits could have seemed downright unmannerly in a tightly built neighborhood. These houses look their best in open, natural settings, especially when there's a spectacular view. Although the Shingle Style never quite managed to wriggle out of the hands of the architects and

into the vernacular building stock, a lot of suburban buildings show signs of having at least brushed up against the idea.

Like the Romanesque, Shingle Style houses are set on heavy masonry foundations. Like the Queen Anne, they are usually large, rambling, "picturesque" buildings. Their roofs may be gabled (like the Queen Anne), hipped, or gambrel (double-pitched as in the Colonial Revival), with dormers of any shape. They almost always have verandahs; rounded or polygonal towers and projecting bays are common. Embellishments are most likely to be Colonial Revival in spirit—simple, classical porch columns, small-paned windows, possibly a Palladian window. Sometimes it's a close call as to whether a house is more Queen Anne or Shingle Style, and then only the all-enveloping wooden shingles on the roof and upper storeys settle the question in favor of Shingle Style.

The differences are also striking, however. Where the Queen Anne is angular, the Shingle Style is smooth and flowing. Unity was the guiding principle behind the Shingle Style. The real purpose of the shingled walls is to meld many irregular shapes into an almost seamless mass that is varied, yet unified; orderly, yet free. And it is the hor-

The Gilbert House, built ca. 1902 in Los Angeles, California, is a late but splendid example of Shingle Style on the West Coast. The unusual design places the second and third storeys within a huge shingled gambrel roof, set on top of a stone first floor. Opposite: A Shingle Style house in Cambridge, Massachusetts, with good curving forms and a wide arch over the entrance.

izontal lines of the Shingle Style that capture our attention. There are no cornerboards at the edges of the buildings; instead, rows of shingles seem to wrap themselves around the corners. Bands of windows carry the eye across the facade. Low-arched eyebrow dormers make barely a ripple in the roofline. Often the roof swoops right over a hipped or gabled dormer or extends down onto the upper wall surface.

Where Queen Anne houses appear lively—always changing planes and colors and materials—Shingle Style buildings are calm and assured. The transition from shingled upper walls to ground floors or foundations of stone is usually soft-pedaled. Colors are quiet: dark, muted wood and stone hues.

In the Shingle Style house, as in the Queen

Anne, emphasis shifts toward comfortable, convenient floorplans—informal, more open, spacious, and welcoming. Now windows opened to the best light and the most appealing views; entrance halls, living rooms, and dining rooms began to flow together to serve family and guests in a more casual relationship; kitchens moved closer to the diners. These concepts seem natural enough today, but they were heady stuff in the 19th century.

Late Victorian architecture took its cues from many influences—from medieval English to the Japanese. Filtered through the American experi-

Edna Villa, McKim, Mead and White's house for Issac Bell, was built in 1882–3 in Newport, Rhode Island. A notable early work of the Shingle Style by the then-young architects, the large, rambling, picturesque house with its smooth, shingled form, is archetypical of the style. The rounded porch and small-paned window reveal a kinship with Queen Anne.

ence, many of these influences met in the Shingle Style, as American housing edged its way toward the low-slung lines of Prairie School residences, the Arts & Crafts Movement, and the Bungalow.

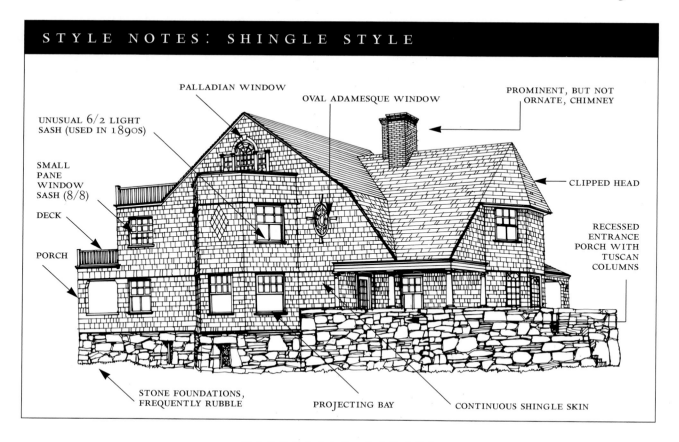

STYLE NOTES: SHINGLE STYLE

PALLADIAN WINDOW

OVAL ADAMESQUE WINDOW

PROMINENT, BUT NOT ORNATE, CHIMNEY

UNUSUAL 6/2 LIGHT SASH (USED IN 1890S)

SMALL PANE WINDOW SASH (8/8)

DECK

PORCH

CLIPPED HEAD

RECESSED ENTRANCE PORCH WITH TUSCAN COLUMNS

STONE FOUNDATIONS, FREQUENTLY RUBBLE

PROJECTING BAY

CONTINUOUS SHINGLE SKIN

MAIL-ORDER DESIGNS

[1875-1940]

I N THE VICTORIAN ERA, the average person hoping for a new home was still at the mercy of his local carpenter/builder and his own training and imagination. Without an architect to direct design and construction, most middle-class houses reflected traditional skills and local building habits more than the owner's personal taste. All that changed, however, with the mass selling of architects' plans by mail. ■ In the late-19th century, this new merchandising technique transformed the house-constuction business and, with it, small cities and towns all across the nation. Spurred by improved technology in printing and transportation, scores of books and periodicals streamed off the presses and into the mailboxes of America's vast army of "intending builders." ■ These publications were churned out in architectural-plan factories by enterprising architects who recognized the value of presenting their work to the broadest possible audience. After all, selling one

The Superintendent's House of the picturesque Hollywood Cemetery, Richmond, Virginia, was executed from George F. Barber's Design No. 61.

design many times promised to be easier than creating a different house for each and every hard-won client. For the first time in history, the common man had a shot at Architecture with a capital A! It was a great leap from single plates in architectural pattern books, or a design in *Godeys Lady's Book*, to full sets of architects' construction blueprints.

Two English-born brothers, George and Charles Palliser, led the way in developing plans by mail. George Palliser was an enormously successful carpenter who had moved up to architecture. In 1876, he issued his first small booklet of plans available by post, *Model Homes for the People, A Complete Guide to the Proper and Economical Erection of Buildings*, which sold out at 25¢. By 1878, he and Charles were partners in Palliser, Palliser & Company, Architects and publishers of *Palliser's American Cottage Homes*.

What made the plans-by-mail idea unique and irresistible was the availability of affordable, full-sized construction drawings prepared by professional architects and accompanied by specifications for materials and techniques, and—best of all—the chance to work with the architect to customize the design. "Keep writing till you get just what you want," urged George F. Barber, one of the most popular of the mail-order architects. "Don't be afraid of writing too often. We are not easily offended."

The John Owings House in Laurens, South Carolina, ca. 1896, is typical of George F. Barber's more flamboyant Eastlake designs. Photo: Jack E. Boucher, HABS. Opposite: Mail-order architect George F. Barber's exuberant Queen Anne Baker House, ca. 1890, in Winchester, Virginia. Barber's houses can sometimes be identified by the many architectural features and projecting corner bays, turrets, and complex gables.

This 1887 shingled and half-timbered Queen Anne in Hyattsville, Maryland, is built from Shoppell's Design No. 444. Opposite: This distinctive design with a projecting partially octagonal front is one of R.W. Shoppell's most characteristic and frequently encountered designs. This example of design #216 is in Gloucester, Massachusetts.

The plan books didn't start any architectural trends. They were intended to echo, not to lead, public opinion in respect to design. After all, the main purpose was to sell plans. "Do not insist on having a very odd or peculiar house," Shoppell admonished his readers. "The best house is one whose exterior and interior are generally approved of by people of good taste."

As for the designs themselves, they ran the gamut of late-19th-century style choices. Barber's were perhaps the most flamboyant, making them among the easiest to spot in today's neighborhoods. Although most of his designs were intended to be built in wood, Barber especially liked the bulky Richardsonian Romanesque style, which most architects built only in brick and stone. His frame houses bustle with rounded wooden bays, turretlike oriels, three-storey towers, many gables, and much carved and turned decoration. Not that he ignored other popular styles: Queen Anne and Colonial Revival details were tossed into the mix with a kind of grand giddiness that today is breathtaking.

R.W. Shoppell and his associates in the Co-Operative Building Plan Association generally favored a quieter aproach with less ornate decoration. Still, they provided plans for massive Queen Anne or Shingle Style buildings with complex, asymmetrical facades and rooflines and plenty of Colonial Revival details.

Thousands of these long-distance dream houses still exist. Can they be identified? Sometimes. On occasion, a house matches a published plan perfectly. More likely, the plan was altered in the building phase; or added to, simplified, modernized, mutilated, or repaired beyond recognition sometime in its hundred-year career. Owners who want to verify the plan-book origins of their 19th-century

Sears Argyle model in Arlington, Virginia. This popular model was in production form 1916 to 1926. Opposite: A Sears Bellewood model, built in Garrett Park, Maryland, in 1931 with a chimney added to the living room on the left.

residences should first gain a good understanding of the range of design sources. The most telling evidence, however, comes from documents, and plans for a particular house.

Plans-by-mail continued into the 20th century and up to this very day, in fact, provide a continuing source of building plans. At the turn of the century designers such as Radford, Hodgson, and Hopkins provided popular designs and in the 1920s there was the American Institute of Architects-sponsored Architects' Small Home Service Bureau, and the Home Owners Service Institute, among many plans providers or suppliers.

Ready-Cut Houses

READY-CUT HOUSES WERE A GIANT STEP BEYOND THE HOUSE plans and stock building parts and millwork of the late 19th century. Ready-cut houses were erected on the building site from lumber that had been cut to size and carefully fitted at the catalog-company's mills. Everything from nails to paint, shingles, and mantelpieces (except, generally, those of masonry) was shipped from the catalog-company's mills and storehouses. All the parts were numbered, and detailed instructions accompanied each order. Homeowners were encouraged to do the con-

struction themselves, alone or with a local builder, carefully following directions and blueprints. And, when the house was finished, some companies, like Sears and Montgomery Ward, stood ready to provide the appliances and furniture, even the china and linens, needed to make the ready-built house totally livable. It was an irresistible idea for an expanding, house-hungry population in economic boom times.

The first precut home company was Aladdin in 1906, followed by Sears, Roebuck in 1908. House sales were specially fruitful in the Midwest, the cradle of American mail-order merchandising as well as a prime source of lumber. Sears, Roebuck and Company and Montgomery Ward, both based in Chicago, and Aladdin Home Company in Bay City, Michigan, were the most active precut house suppliers on a national level, but

The ever-popular Cape Cod in a Sears design, the "Attleboro," built in Madison, New Jersey, a model produced from 1933 to 1939. Opposite: Sears's popular "Conway" model in Cheverly, Maryland, was in production from 1926 to 1933.

there were scores of other smaller, regional or local companies all over the country, including Bennett and Lewis Homes for example.

Homeowner response to the well-built little houses was enthusiastic. And no wonder: The savings in building costs seems to have been substantial, and the building materials came with ironclad guarantees of quality. Sears claimed a savings in labor costs of $500 on a $1,650 house, and guaranteed its lumber as knot-free. Aladdin offered "a dollar a knot" for any flaws that could be found in its building lumber.

This wasn't avant-garde architecture, although much of it was highly competent. Ready-built houses, like ready-made house plans, were adapted from the most familiar—the most "homey"—of the academic architectural trends of the late-19th and early-20th centuries. Some pop-

ular models remained available (and sought after) for many years. There were a few basic house types—Bungalows, cottages, Foursquares, and Homestead houses—built in broadly interpreted decorative styles: Colonial Revival (mostly English in feeling, but often Dutch); Craftsman (sometimes with a Prairie touch); and a few historical European styles, such as English Tudor cottages, French farmhouses or Spanish missions. Colonial Revival houses and Cape Cod cottages eventually triumphed by the late 1930s.

Enormous numbers of precut houses still stand. Although a good number have been considerably altered and enlarged over the years, they are mostly in great shape, thanks to a good start.

So how can you tell whether yours is a Sears (or an Aladdin, WardWay, Liberty, or Lewis) home? Tracing provenance is not always easy, given the number of similar designs sold. What looks like an Aladdin house might well have been supplied by Sears, or vice versa. Furthermore, buyers were encouraged to make minor changes in their plans, particularly to reverse floor plans and to add porches and extra rooms. However, many of these relatively recent houses are still in the hands of the original owners or their families, so it's sometimes possible to find copies of plans, specifications, or purchase or mortgage papers.

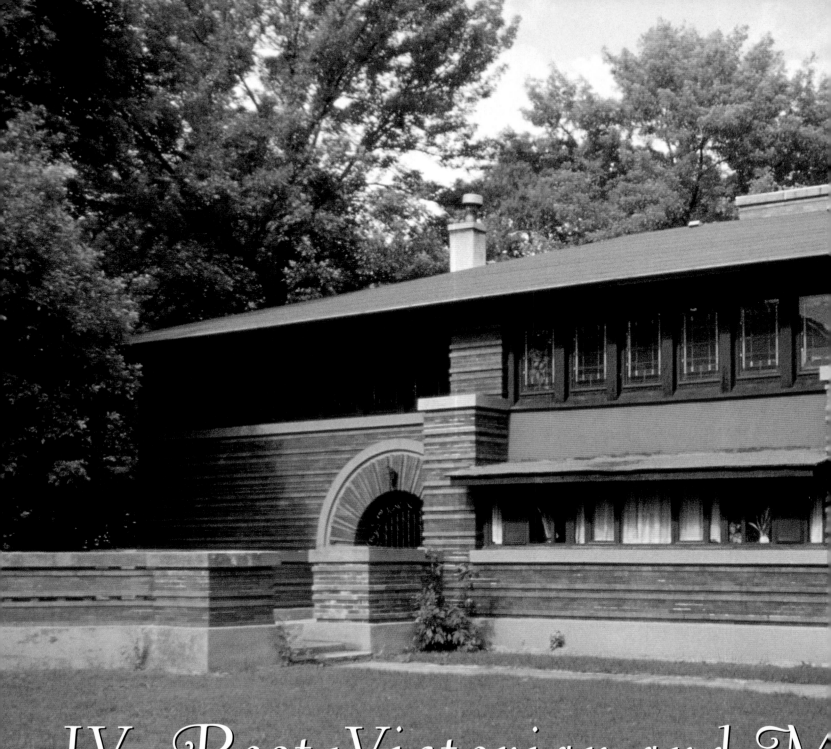

IV. Post-Victorian and M

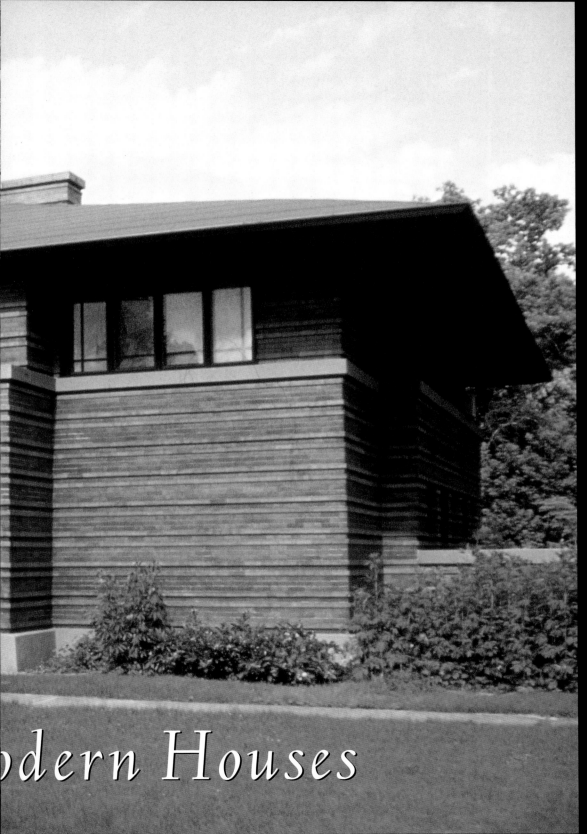

odern Houses

BEAUX ARTS

[1880-1940]

NEARLY ALL AMERICAN architectural styles begin at the top and sift downward from expensive architect-designed, high-style houses to the homes of the less-than-wealthy. Gothic and Greek Revival details, for instance, turn up as frequently in small farmhouses as in great city mansions. One grand exception to the trickle-down rule is Academic Eclecticism, also known as the Beaux Arts or American Renaissance style. ■ Strictly speaking, however, none of these terms really refers to any particular "style," but to a way of thinking about styles. Although it drew most heavily from Italian and French Renaissance design sources, Academic Eclecticism was influenced by many other historical European styles and periods as well. The peak of its popularity spanned the years from about 1890 until about 1917. ■ As applied to houses, Academic Eclecticism belonged to the very rich. It called for

Beaux Arts principles are softly stated with a Mediterranean air in The Flagler Mansion, Palm Beach, Florida. It was designed in 1901 by Carrère and Hastings, architects for the railroad magnate.

large, formal, expensive homes that were nearly always built of masonry and adorned with a great deal of sophisticated, carved, classical ornament.

THE SEEDS OF ACADEMIC ECLECTICISM WERE SOWN IM-mediately after the Civil War, when would-be American architects traveled abroad to study in European *ateliers*, particularly at l'Ecole des Beaux Arts in Paris. By the end of the century, an entire generation of architects had been trained at l'Ecole, by Beaux Arts professors in American schools, or by Beaux Arts architectural offices in this country. It was, in fact, the first generation of professionally trained architects in the nation's history, and they were at work in the United States.

Their restraint was a far cry from the grab-bag approach of the late-Victorian era, when the rush was on to identify the one, true "American style." This time, architects were not looking for a style as such, but for a way of integrating the best architecture of the past with modern uses, needs, materials, and technology. They did not want to copy European buildings so much as interpret them for a modern American audience.

All this might have remained no more than high-flown theory had it not been for the World's

Columbian Exposition held in Chicago in 1893. The Beaux Arts-style exposition buildings were arranged in a lakefront grouping dubbed the "White City," a dazzling—and temporary—Never-Never-Land free of the poverty, filth, and disorder that plagued Chicago and other American cities. The buildings represented an ideal of urban beauty that struck a chord with the general public as well as with the architectural community. Could Americans become better, happier, healthier citizens simply by being exposed to beautiful public places? Why not?

Optimism reigned, and similar expositions were organized in other cities, spreading the gospel of the City Beautiful throughout the land, where

The garden facade of Edwin Berwind's Newport, Rhode Island, summer home interprets rather than copies the small chateau on which it was modeled. The Elms, by Horace Trumbauer. Opposite: This group of three New York City houses on Fifth Avenue facing Central Park shows the Beaux Arts town house at its most polished. A unified cornice line and rounded bays on the end houses provide an air of high sophistication in design. Thorne House was designed by C.P.H. Gilbert in 1902. The mansard roof continued to be used on French-inspired Beaux Arts designs.

it was eagerly received by civic leaders, architects, and the public. Almost overnight, Victorian

libraries, post offices, railroad stations, courthouses, city halls, and university buildings are Academic Eclecticism's most visible monuments. However, it was equally useful for houses, from large, freestanding mansions to smaller, but still sizable, attached townhouses, especially in cities like Boston, New York, Chicago, St. Louis, San Francisco, and Washington. Suburban examples were less common, and small-town examples are nearly nonexistent.

Rich materials, elegantly handled, were the hallmarks of these substantial houses. They were nearly always built of masonry, often of smooth, light-colored, ashlar-cut limestone. There was invariably an impressive, formal front entrance, usually with elaborate carving around the doorway. On the most pretentious buildings, the carved ornament stretched from foundation to chimney caps, as reclining cherubim, flower-filled urns, or other statuary adorned overdoors, cornices, or spandrels. Columns in the classical orders were extensively used in colonnades across the fronts of buildings,

designs became outdated, and the emerging Modern and Prairie styles were stopped virtually dead in their tracks. Only Academic Eclecticism, it seemed clear, could build the City Beautiful.

THE BEAUX ARTS MODE WORKED ESPECIALLY WELL FOR large public and institutional structures. In the early-20th-century drive toward social improvement, practically every town of any size had at least one such building on the drawing board. Thus

as supports for arches and porches, or as colonnettes grouped beneath the pediments of dormers. Balustrades of wrought iron or stone paraded across the tops of buildings.

Town houses were usually built in three or four bays and were three or four storeys tall (frequently five storeys in New York). A low ground floor or "basement" provided service areas and entrances, but the real attention was centered one floor up, on the "first" floor, or *piano nobile*, where guests were entertained and families gathered. Often a mansard roof accommodated an extra half-storey at the top, particularly in French-inspired designs. Hipped or flat roofs were common in Italian models.

As context was everything, grounds and gardens were vital to the success of a Beaux Arts house. Large formal gardens, arranged with an eye to axial symmetry, were as carefully furnished and decorated as the rooms of the house. Classical sculpture, fountains, parterres, and painstakingly arranged vistas from one section of the garden to the next delighted the visitor and kept gardeners busy.

If the exteriors were grand, the interiors were likely to be breathtaking. Commanding staircases of marble with wrought-iron railings, specifically designed to allow theatrical entrances to social or state affairs, wound their way to the upper storeys. Coffered ceilings with elaborate figural paintings and plaster moldings and cornices teased the eye upward. Walls were often paneled in fine woods or painted with classical murals. Massive mantelpieces in marble or wood were more for ostenta-

Distinctively from the tradition of the Italian Renaissance, the Joseph Beale House in Washington, D.C., is remarkable for its curving swell front and the colossal second-floor Palladian window. Designed in 1907–8 by Glenn Brown, it now houses the Embassy of Egypt.

tious display than for warmth.

The floor plans provided for masculine rooms and feminine rooms, rooms for sleeping, dressing, and bathing. There were formal dining rooms and smaller breakfast rooms; sitting rooms for intimate chats; salons for chatting with worthy strangers; morning rooms and solariums; music rooms, game rooms, and billiard rooms. There were offices and service areas, servants' quarters, laundries, kitchens, and butlers' pantries. Not necessarily all of these rooms were in every house, of course, but there were usually enough rooms to make moving easily from one part of the house to another something of a problem for the servants, of whom there were a great many. So floor plans required special attention to make sure they remained stylishly symmetrical, yet allowed efficient circulation by family, staff, and guests.

The City Beautiful Movement did not transform every American city into a place of beauty and harmony, but it did change most of then permanently for the better. And Academic Eclecticism, while it could not provide a home for Everyman, did provide a standard for beauty and order that is still part of our national consciousness.

COLONIAL REVIVAL

[1890-1940]

T HE MOST POPULAR ARCHITECTURAL STYLE in America's history, the Colonial Revival, took root in the late 1870s and has continued to flourish into the present. The closing years of the 1800s were a period of architectural richness, with the Queen Anne and Shingle styles showing signs of great and enduring popularity while the Eastlake and Stick styles vied for minor roles on the architectural stage. In the midst of all this bustle, a sudden wave of nostalgic patriotism and a yearning for old-time simplicity swept the country. Inspired in part by the United States Centennial celebration of 1876, it was heightened by the shocking loss of American shrines, such as the celebrated John Hancock House, demolished in 1863. As their nation matured, Victorian Americans began to take an interest in its past, particularly in the "good old days" before the fast-moving Industrial

In the 1930s Colonial Revival homes became less ornate than earlier examples. The roof is lower, and the lines are more restrained. This prototypical example is at Fort Belvoir, Virginia, and is an excellent example of a 1935 military house.

Revolution had wrought its scary mix of technological wonders and horrors. National pride mingled with a feeling that things seemed to be moving a little too fast for comfort at the end of the nation's first century. No wonder, critics noted, that people were ready to step back a hundred years or so into a quieter, less hectic world.

Late-Victorian architecture was ready for a change as well. The simple English, German, and Dutch dwellings of the colonial past seemed more and more attractive when viewed beside the overdecorated, all-too-picturesque houses of the

Some houses came close to copying the originals as with this 1920s house in Washington, D.C., directly inspired by Woodlawn Plantation, the Federal-style mansion in Mount Vernon, Virginia. Opposite: The early Colonial Revival is a blend of late Queen Anne and 18th-century details, as the James P. Tierney House (1905) in Providence, Rhode Island, demonstrates. The hip roof, dormers, arched doorway, and handsome Ionic rounded entrance porch with balustrade are clearly based on 18th-century design motifs, rather than Queen Anne.

Victorian era. But while colonial houses were admirable, they were also, by Victorian standards, usually much too small and excessively plain, not to mention technologically backward. They had none of the modern comforts, such as central heating, large-paned windows, and conveniently located and equipped kitchens, that had become standard in late-19th-century homes. Architectural simplicity was one thing, but those early houses had no bays or turrets at all—and no verandahs!

American homeowners were in the mood for a Colonial Revival, but only on their own terms. The Queen Anne house would have to go, but the country was not about to give up the expansive interiors, flexible floor plans, interesting building shapes, and big porches it had so recently taken to its heart. Obviously, Yankee ingenuity could be counted on to bring colonial architecture into the

new era. By combining Queen Anne features with Georgian and Federal-style ornament, an acceptable new colonial style was sure to evolve in due time.

And evolve it did. It was helped along by a reawakened interest in classicism among many of the nation's young architects, who were being trained in, or greatly influenced by, the rigorous tradition of France's Ecole des Beaux Arts. They learned to apply the concepts of architectural historicism to American building—particularly to the Georgian and Federal-style houses being

A popular entry porch in the early 20th century featured paired narrow columns supporting a pediment with an arched head echoing a colonial sash door with an arched transom. This house in Washington, D.C., uses the familiar dressed rubble stonework of the Mid-Atlantic states. Opposite: This 1902 frame house in Providence, Rhode Island, blends the large-scale multiple bay windows and ample verandah of the Queen Anne, with distinct 18th-century colonial features: the gambrel roof detail, the molded eaves cornice, and the modillion verandah cornice. Victorian gingerbread has been banished in the rush to embrace the colonial.

The master of the picturesque Pennsylvania stone-farmhouse revival was R. Brognard Okie, whose own house of ca. 1930 is in Devon, Pennsylvania.

rediscoverd in towns such as Newport, Rhode Island, and Salem, Massachussetts.

Charles McKim of McKim, Mead & White led the way in the late 1870s by embarking with other members of his firm on a well-publicized tour of New England's historic houses, measuring and sketching all the way. Their success encouraged others, both professional architects and talented amateurs, to document old houses in other regions. Architects were urged to study "humbly and earnestly" the principles that shaped building in the colonial period, not just as a way to pick up quaint details to be copied in modern buildings, but in order to learn how the forms had evolved

and how they could best be used to serve the new age. Architects such as Arthur Little, Herbert Browne, Robert Peabody, John Stearns, Glenn Brown, and George Mason, Jr., turned a serious eye on colonial dwellings.

Nonetheless, very few of the earliest Colonial Revival houses came anywhere near being "archaeologically" correct. For one thing, they were much larger than their colonial antecedents, although the shapes generally were simpler and more rectangular than Queen Anne houses, with far fewer towers and projecting bays. Georgian symmetry returned to the facade. At first, ornament tended to be overscaled and not particularly accurate adaptations of colonial decoration. Gradually, however, exterior trim acquired a more restrained, classical form, with Adamesque swags in gabled pediments and modillion and dentil trim at the cornice lines. Porches began to replace verandahs, and both were likely to be supported by columns in the unadorned Tuscan or Ionic mode. Rooflines were simplified, as straightforward gables, gambrels, and hipped roofs served this less flamboyant era well. Prominent chimneys were less frequently used and generally less important than in Queen Anne houses.

One or, at most, two building materials—

An attractive Southern mixture of Victorian Queen Anne and Georgian formality, with the typical oversized roof and 18th-century details. This design still featured a wraparound verandah and rounded corner bay of the previous era. This house of ca. 1900 is in Camden, South Carolina.

The Colonial Revival architects quickly mastered the revival of their 18th-century models. This typical early-20th-century example in Kansas City, Missouri, is like many from coast to coast, and is a bolder design than those that followed in the 1930s.

wood, brick, or stone, simply handled—seemed more suitable than multiple siding materials. Doorways were the focal point of the facade, just as they had been in colonial days, with elaborate columned and pilastered surrounds, while fanlights with delicate tracery replaced the flashy stained-glass transoms of earlier days.

Interiors were changing too. Although floor plans remained flexible, the traditional center hall made its return, and decorative elements quieted down. Staircases assumed elegant, gently curving

handrails with simple turned balusters. Fireplaces were no less coveted in turn-of-the-century Colonial Revival houses than those built during the Queen Anne's heyday, but they were now more likely to be flanked by delicate classical pilasters and

A popular variation in the Colonial Revival was the Dutch Colonial, as in this example in Ridgewood, New Jersey. The principal features of the Dutch Colonial are a gambrel roof, sometimes, as here, with a kick at the eaves extending out over the facade, and the second-floor front showing a continuous frame "dormer."

surmounted by paneled overmantels than surrounded by fancy tilework and mirrors in heavy carved and varnished frames.

The Colonial Revival style maintained its popularity well into the 20th century, becoming simpler with each passing decade. Naturally, the wealthy of the era required larger and more elaborate houses, but architects found it easy to enlarge and repeat the original modestly sized colonial building unit until an appropriate size was achieved for their well-heeled clients.

But it was the new middle class that made the Colonial Revival the architectural star of the 20th century. By the time of the great post–World War I building boom of the 1920s and 1930s, it was the most important of the many revival styles that

formed America's huge new suburbs. Colonial Revival houses and small Cape Cods filled the catalogs of mass producers of house plans and ready-cut houses, filling the needs of the middle class. These later Colonial Revival houses were small and simple, closer to the scale of their Early American prototypes. Colonial Revival details found their way even into Foursquares and Bungalows, the other middle-class power houses of the early 20th century.

As the decades wore on, suburban streetscapes took on an increasingly sedate air. Blocks of

The early-20th-century suburb was home to many fine Colonial and Georgian Revival houses, such as the George B. Kennedy House in the Alexandria, Virginia, suburb of Rosemont; Waddy Wood, architect, 1916.

unassuming Colonial Revival buildings filled pleasant neighborhoods where the houses seemed to share a comfortable family resemblance. Variety for the sake of variety had been replaced by a subtle and, to the millions of Americans who lived in such homes, deeply satisfying traditionalism.

STYLE NOTES: COLONIAL REVIVAL

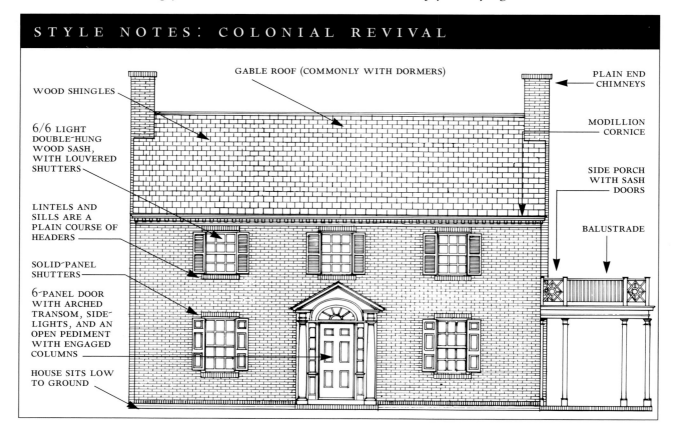

GABLE ROOF (COMMONLY WITH DORMERS)

PLAIN END CHIMNEYS

WOOD SHINGLES

MODILLION CORNICE

6/6 LIGHT DOUBLE-HUNG WOOD SASH, WITH LOUVERED SHUTTERS

SIDE PORCH WITH SASH DOORS

LINTELS AND SILLS ARE A PLAIN COURSE OF HEADERS

BALUSTRADE

SOLID-PANEL SHUTTERS

6-PANEL DOOR WITH ARCHED TRANSOM, SIDE-LIGHTS, AND AN OPEN PEDIMENT WITH ENGAGED COLUMNS

HOUSE SITS LOW TO GROUND

Bungalows & Arts & Crafts

[1890-1920]

IN BRITAIN, THE ARTS & CRAFTS MOVEMENT was a protest against Victorian fussiness. As socialist thinkers and reformers, its adherents deplored the industrial processes of the period, which they considered dehumanizing to the laboring class. They found the products "dishonest" and "insincere" in the way materials were used. In their minds, the way to improve the popular taste and restore dignity, joy, and morality to work and home was to reorganize craftsmen into guilds that produced handmade items under humane working conditions. ▪ Consequently, designer William Morris and others set up a number of guildlike establishments in which many beautiful and tasteful objects were made and sold to those who were rich and discerning enough to buy them. Delightful brick and half-timbered country estates were built for the landed gentry. But the lot of the laboring man was not much improved, and neither was his aesthetic sense. ▪ From

Half-timbered and stuccoed houses were a big favorite with East Coast architects; this one is in Madison, New Jersey. Note the mix of casements and double-hung sash.

the late 1890s until World War I, the Arts & Crafts Movement received enthusiastic support from groups of forward-thinking young American architects, furniture makers, and social reformers. Americans made pilgrimages to England and

Scotland. While the dream of returning to an earlier ethic of work and art may have been the same on both sides of the Atlantic, the practical effects were very different. In Britain, professional Arts & Crafts architects catered to a small, upper-class clientele. In the United States, however, Arts & Crafts architecture was a widespread and highly successful response to middle-class demand for affordable, efficient, and attractive suburban homes.

Distinctive regional variations in the United States soon appeared. In the Northeast, architects such as Philadelphia's Wilson Eyre designed mansions with half-timbering and steeply pitched roofs in the British manner. In the Midwest, Frank

Opposite: At Cape May, New Jersey, this two-storey house has strong Craftsman features such as a two-storey front porch, interlocking triple porch posts, and broad eaves with dormers on triangular struts. It is a model, early-20th-century seashore house. Below: Bernard Maybeck's San Francisco houses are a distinctive blend of Arts & Crafts with flamboyant decorative features, such as the Gothic tracery on the Roos House balcony of 1909.

In Pasadena, California, in the David B. Gamble House of 1908, architects Greene and Greene produced the best of California Arts & Crafts houses, a blend that included Craftsman and Japanese influences and included beautifully detailed exposed wood framing interlocked and seemingly pegged together. The numerous porches were functional; each bedroom had its own sleeping porch.

Lloyd Wright and his colleagues of the up-and-coming Prairie School led the way, building low, sweeping, horizontal houses for wealthy Chicago suburbanites that seemed worlds removed from the skyscrapers being built downtown. On the West Coast, Charles Sumner Greene and his brother Henry Mather Greene blended Spanish and Oriental elements to produce a high-style wooden architecture unique to California.

Gustav Stickley

BUT IT WAS A FURNITURE MAKER-TURNED-PUBLISHER named Gustav Stickley who brought Arts & Crafts architecture to the middle class. Stickley began publishing *The Craftsman*, a popular magazine filled with philosophy and furniture designs, in 1901. The magazine, which continued until 1916, was intended partly to advertise his company's line of simple, blocky furniture with good proportions and solid construction. But just as important, to Stickley's mind, it was an opportunity to spread the Arts & Crafts creed. Stickley hoped that Arts & Crafts furnishings and, almost as an afterthought, ap-

propriate houses to put them in would point the way to a return to simpler values and a happier life for the common man.

Stickley hired professionals (usually not identified in print) to design houses for the magazine. He also ran articles and house designs by architects in other parts of the country, such as the California firms of Greene & Greene and Irving Gill. In January 1904, the first in a series of monthly house plans was offered, free of charge, to subscribers to *The Craftsman*'s new Home Builders Club; these plans would eventually number over 200. The houses, which were expected to cost between $2,000 and $15,000, featured open interior floorplans and were clearly aimed at the middle-class family. *The Craftsman* had entered the competitive

A major manifestation of the Arts & Crafts era was Art Nouveau, almost completely a European style. The entry to Mineral Hall, the R.E. Bruner House in Kansas City, Missouri, 1903–4, is one of the few examples of this style in the United States. This is one of the most distinctive designs of Lewis Curtis.

world of the mail-order architect—but Stickley was giving his designs away. He even offered free advice to homebuilders who wanted to modify the plans. He also published detailed plans for furniture similar to those his company sold and gave free advice to woodworkers who used the designs.

"Style" is almost too strong a word for the exterior design of many Craftsman houses. On the outside, they displayed a variety of unpretentious architectural forms. They borrowed from the English Arts & Crafts, the American Shingle Style, and the Colonial Revival. However, Stickley and *The Craftsman* played a major role in popularizing the Bungalow, by far the hottest house type of the early 20th century.

The Virtue of Simplicity

THE IMPORTANT CONCEPT BEHIND A CRAFTSMAN HOUSE was that it had to be perfectly suited to the use for which it was intended. The exterior design followed as a matter of course and was always simple, appropriate to its suburban or rural setting,

and honest in its use of materials. Consequently, there were a lot of Foursquares, some very simple T- and L-shaped houses, and an occasional U built around a patio, popular in California.

The small amount of decoration that was used expressed structural consideration. Exposed rafter ends were almost a Craftsman trademark. Symmetry for symmetry's sake was frowned upon; symmetry for simplicity's sake was encouraged. Enormous stone or brick exterior chimneys suggested a broad

A fine small house may have been called either a Bungalow or a cottage. This well-proportioned example is in Saginaw, Michigan.

This classic form of Bungalow has a low sweeping roof that extends down over the front porch, as does the house in the Rosemont district of Alexandria, Virginia. Accented by ribbon shed dormers and battered porch posts, it is easy to see why this is a house type that America found easy to like.

hearth and a warm and happy family life within.

Fresh air and sunshine were considered essential to health and comfort, and so there had to be at least one outdoor "room" for fair-weather dining, sitting, or visiting. And there had to be a porch, and often a pergola as well. Frequently there were sleeping porches. Gardens and landscaping were integral to the design.

Although Craftsman plans always suggested appropriate building materials, homeowners were expected to make their own choices from what was readily available and economical in the area. Ideally, they would use materials found or pro-

duced near the building site, and were urged to use the best they could afford and to finish them with care. "Natural" Craftsman materials included wood-shingled walls and wooden rafters, sturdy stone foundations, lower storeys of smooth rounded stones, stuccoed or cement wall finishes, concrete walls and columns, rough-textured, multicolored brick, and Spanish or flat-tile or slate roofs. Stickley himself had a weakness for log houses.

But it was the interior that mattered most. An open floor plan brought family and guests together in combination stairhalls/living rooms, while inglenooks, windowseats, and artfully planned recesses encouraged private activities such as reading. To minimize maintenance and housekeeping, the rooms were sparsely furnished, preferably with built-ins and a few freestanding pieces purchased from Stickley's firm or built by the homeowner from the free plans published in *The Craftsman*. Again, decorative interest was supplied by the use of natural materials—stone, brick, glazed tiles, copper, bronze, and lots and lots of richly colored wood in paneling, floors, and built-in furnishings.

Bungalows

FROM 1900 UNTIL WORLD WAR I, NO HOUSE EXCITED the American homeowner's imagination more than the Bungalow. It seemed the perfect small house, and it was tirelessly promoted and enthusiastically built even in areas where its warm-weather ori-

gins were not particularly apt. (The name seems to have come from "bangala" or Bengali, and originally indicated a form of summer house used by colonists in India.) Architects such as Charles and Henry Greene in California made it high style, and Prairie School architects embroidered on Bungalow characteristics, but it was the American public who made it, with its open floor-plan and one-floor living, a mainstay of early-20th-century suburbs.

Fred T. Hodgson, the editor of *Hodgson's Practical Bungalows and Cottages* (Chicago: Frederick J.

This Craftsman-influenced Bungalow in Coronado, California, has both porch and pergola. The massive rounded stone piers and short, battered wooden posts complement deeply projecting joists at the corners.

Drake & Co., 1906), called it "the best type of cheap frame house which has been erected in large numbers in this country since the old New England farmhouse went out of fashion." Of course, Hodgson may have had an eye to selling his Bungalow house plans. Not everyone agreed with Hodgson's assessment of its merits, however. Some critics called it "the least house for the most money," a reference to the inordinate amount of lot area it occupied. Most Bungalow owners, however, probably would have agreed with Hodgson's explanation of the building's charm: "There is nothing either affected or insincere about these little houses. They are neither consciously artistic nor consciously rustic. They are the simple and unconscious expression of the needs of their owners, and as such they can be credited with the best kind of architectural propriety."

The true Bungalow is a relatively long, low, one- or one-and-one-half-storey building with a con-

spicuous roof, overhanging eaves, and an ample front porch included under the main roof structure. Built snug to the ground, it was intended to relate in scale and color to the surrounding shrubbery and tress. Ideally, indoors and out were blended to encourage relaxed communication between the inhabitants and nature.

The Bungalow is usually covered either with shingles or shakes (large, rough shingles) in natural earth-tone colors, although sometimes clapboard or stucco were used. The emphasis is on plain, straightforward design and materials, and a warm domesticity. It is hard to think of a Bungalow

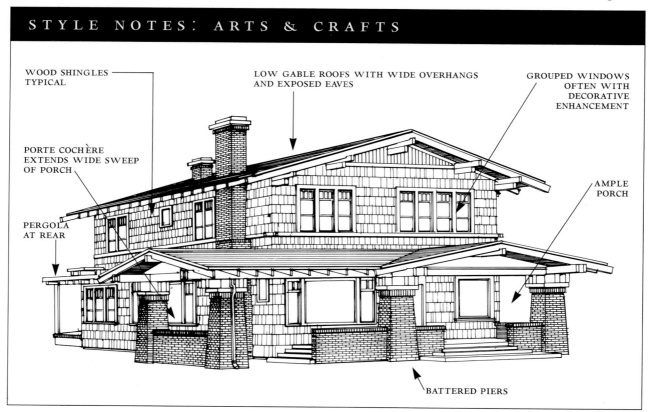

STYLE NOTES: ARTS & CRAFTS

WOOD SHINGLES TYPICAL

LOW GABLE ROOFS WITH WIDE OVERHANGS AND EXPOSED EAVES

GROUPED WINDOWS OFTEN WITH DECORATIVE ENHANCEMENT

PORTE COCHÈRE EXTENDS WIDE SWEEP OF PORCH

AMPLE PORCH

PERGOLA AT REAR

BATTERED PIERS

without its porch—or more often, porches, often including a pergola. The most common type has the familiar long, low sweeping gable roof with open eaves, and perhaps projecting joists to form a continuous surface sheltering the front porch. Porch piers were commonly wood posts, sometimes doubled, sometimes with small round cobblestone bases. The stone may also appear in the foundation or interior fireplace. Piers and posts are often battered or sloped.

Dormer windows—usually a ribbon of them—were common. Occasionally one encounters a two-storey Bungalow, called by builders of the time a semi-Bungalow. On the side of the house, the porch may extend to become a *porte cochère*, covering the auto entrance, or a pergola, sheltering a

An unusual two-storey Craftsman Bungalow in Pensacola, Florida, with cross gables and deep-bracketed eaves sheltering a corner porch on brick piers. The facade-wide strip of ten windows is a distinctive feature.

sunny area. Although the Bungalow is most readily identified with California, it is commonly found in all regions of the country.

Builders in the teens and twenties drew a fine line between the Bungalow form and the cottage. Both are one- or one-and-a-half-storey buildings. There is frequently a larger upstairs in the cottage, and cottages are more vertically oriented than Bungalows. Cottages are a traditional vernacular building type that sometimes have Colonial-era details.

THE PRAIRIE STYLE

[1897-1921]

AMERICA'S SUBURBS ABOUNDED with Queen Anne-style peaks and turrets and machine-made ornament in the 1890s, but an almost unbelievable change was already in the air. For over two centuries we had copied and reinterpreted European styles and periods. Now an entirely new architecture—one that we still call "modern"—came to life on our Midwestern prairies. On the outskirts of Chicago, a group of young architects led by Frank Lloyd Wright was rethinking American building for the 20th century. Having helped produce the ultimate symbol of life in the industrial age, the skyscraper, these Midwesterners were ready to redefine the most basic building type, the house. ■ The Prairie School unofficially began in 1897, when Frank Lloyd Wright, Dwight Perkins, Robert Spencer, and Marion Hunt formed a coterie at Chicago's Steinway Hall. The Chicago School, as the move-

Davenport House, River Forest, Illinois. Frank Lloyd Wright, 1901. A very early example of Wright's development of the modern house, this facade seems caught in time halfway between a late-Victorian house and one in Wright's mature style.

ment initially was known, encompassed both sky-scrapers and houses—not illogical, as many architects worked in both fields. Later, however, the term Chicago School was reserved for commercial-building designs, and Prairie Style or Prairie School was used to describe residential work. Considering its lasting impact and worldwide renown—it was the first American architectural effort to be taken seriously in Europe—the Prairie School was short-lived in the United States. It flourished from 1900 until the beginning of the first world war, and then lost out to the fashion for revival styles, particularly the "Early American" Colonial Revival, in the post-war building boom. It never became a

Bernard Corrigan House, Kansas City, Missouri. Lewis Curtis, 1912–13. An outstanding work by one of several Prairie architects practicing outside the Chicago area, it's a powerful and creative house that still manages to blend with more traditional houses of its period. Opposite: Edward R. Hills House, Oak Park, Illinois. Frank Lloyd Wright, 1906.

predominant style, although it had plenty of middle-class followers, particularly from Minnesota to Iowa.

The low Prairie house must have looked alien to eyes accustomed to mainstream architecture.

Frank Lloyd Wright's redefinition of the house was complete with the Robie house of 1908–9 in Chicago, Illinois. It skillfully combined indoor and outdoor spaces while opening up the interior as a functional whole—on a narrow corner city lot.

Easterners generally chose rather traditional Colonial Revival or European-inspired Beaux Arts-style houses in which to live. On the West Coast, those who wanted a change looked to the California Bungalow. In the Midwest, however, where cities were booming, there was a fresh crop of architects and clients who were open to new ideas not influenced by European historical precedents and formal architectural training.

With an emphasis on fitting architecture into the environment, the final form Prairie houses took is not surprising. Because prairies are flat, it followed that Prairie houses should be built low to the ground. Horizontal lines were punctuated by vertical elements—big chimneys, masonry piers, and tall casement windows—just as the prairie's horizon is broken by an occasional tree. The low roofline might be hipped, flat, or gabled, but it usually had wide overhanging eaves and enclosed rafters that provided shelter from the harsh prairie winds. There was no basement (unhealthy) or attic (inefficient). The general effect was likely to be that of a "high-waisted" building, with the visual emphasis placed on the top half of the second-floor level, accentuated by string courses or horizontal wood trim. The sturdy, square pillars that anchored

the entrance and the corners of the building became almost a cliché of Prairie Style design.

Like Craftsman houses, Prairie houses claimed honesty in the choice of building materials. In contrast to the picturesque jumble of materials found in Queen Anne buildings, Prairie architects used a single building material whenever possible. Wood and stucco were employed for economy's sake, but masonry was preferred, particularly streamlined Roman brick in light colors.

Of the architects associated with the Prairie School, Frank Lloyd Wright was preeminent. The citizens of a democracy, Wright declared, needed "something better than [a] box" in which to live. So

This solid, somewhat traditional Prairie design house of ca. 1905 in Kenilworth, Illinois, is typical of George W. Maher's work.

he set out to dismantle the old, cold box to make way for a warm, "organic" architecture. Despite its distinctive exterior appearance, the real achievement of the Prairie house lay in its freed-up floorplan and the way it made walls, inside and out, seem to disappear. At its best, the Prairie house was not a collection of walls defining empty spaces, but flowing space that deemphasized the surrounding walls. Windows were no longer simply holes punched into walls, but "light screens" that invited the outdoors in. Interior walls gave way to head-high movable partitions that allowed air, light, and people to circulate freely. Without walls, one centrally placed chimney was enough to warm the whole house, physically and psychologically. The Prairie house was more than a "style"—it was a revolution in the design of living spaces.

Wright's personal life, always subject to unexpected detours, led him to Europe for an extended spell in 1910, and later to Japan and California. The Prairie School did not just dry up and blow away with Wright's departure, however (although he was known to propagate such an idea). It continued to flourish as other architects found the limelight and developed their own styles.

The Prairie-house concept was spread by pattern books, published in the Midwest and distributed nationally, which offered plans at low prices. A good example is Radford's *Cement Houses and How to Build Them* (The Radford Architectural Company, Chicago, 1909), which presented several designs that nicely blended Prairie styling with early-20th-century building technology. Many houses built from pattern-book plans or designed by local architects are scattered about the country. The favorite vernacular was a Foursquare with an off-center entrance and hipped roof.

Prairie houses shared some general charac-

Designed by William Drummond in 1910, his own house in River Forest, Illinois, is a classic example of Prairie Style.

teristics with Stickley's Craftsman homes and Greene & Greene's California Bungalows: simple exteriors, functional floor plans, integration of house and environment, and an emphasis on horizontal lines and wide eaves. There was also a common interest in carefully finished interiors featuring natural woods, often set into panels on plastered walls; large fireplaces, frequently surrounded by richly colored, unpatterned tilework; and an overall emphasis on human scale.

Although the first Prairie School houses were sometimes laid out symmetrically, they became more asymmetrical as the style developed. In fact,

Opposite: Reverend J. R. Ziegler House, Frankfort, Kentucky. Frank Lloyd Wright, 1909. A typical, developed Wright approach for a narrow, urban lot.

the later floor plans were often created in the shape of a cross or a somewhat irregular T. Inside, the ideal was a flowing, "one-room" floor plan, except where walls were needed for privacy, as in bedrooms and service areas. Porches, terraces, and porte cochères extended the horizontal sweep. Planters and window boxes were a significant part of the design, again intended to integrate inner and outer spaces.

STYLE NOTES: THE PRAIRIE SCHOOL

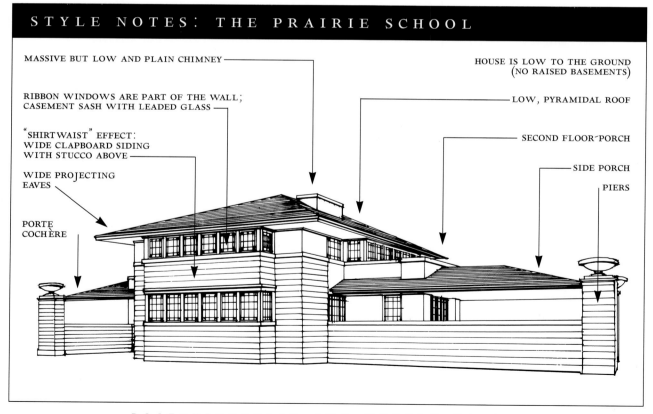

MASSIVE BUT LOW AND PLAIN CHIMNEY

RIBBON WINDOWS ARE PART OF THE WALL; CASEMENT SASH WITH LEADED GLASS

"SHIRTWAIST" EFFECT: WIDE CLAPBOARD SIDING WITH STUCCO ABOVE

WIDE PROJECTING EAVES

PORTE COCHÈRE

HOUSE IS LOW TO THE GROUND (NO RAISED BASEMENTS)

LOW, PYRAMIDAL ROOF

SECOND FLOOR PORCH

SIDE PORCH

PIERS

BUILDER STYLE

[1895-1930]

T HE WORKING-CLASS homes of the late-19th and early-20th centuries—Homesteads, Foursquares, cottages, and Bungalows—are long on function, and short on stylistic effects and architectural grandeur. With their middle-class size and relatively plain finishes, they share a common social context. They were the starter houses of the up-and-coming homeowner class of several generations past. ▪ Because these houses are relatively new, they are great in number. We see them every day. Many of us live in them quite contentedly, for they continue to offer pleasant spaces, generally in pleasant neighborhoods. Those that defy style classification may simply be called Builder Style, a term that pays tribute to the crucial role that speculative developers, plan-book designers, and mail-order houses played in putting homes on the building lots of America's suburbs.

The boxy shape and low-hipped roof are basic to the Foursquare house. This fine example in Frankfurt, Kentucky, shows its Prairie influence with wide, open eaves. It has an unusual set of triple windows on the second floor as well as paired porch columns.

They made home ownership a reality for millions of people from 1895 to 1930.

No one wants to hear that they have a "no-style" house. It's almost like suggesting their baby might not be ... well, beautiful! This is not to say that these houses share no similarities with formal styles. All houses have form. But Builder Style houses are designated so by form rather than by detail. You may notice, for instance, that Builder Style Bungalows, while usually smaller, are shaped pretty much like Arts & Crafts Bungalows. They have low, spreading roofs, front porches with sloping, squared-off piers, maybe even a pergola. However, the Arts & Crafts examples use more ornament and better materials, with an eye toward artistic effect, whereas Builder Style Bungalows forego expensive materials and refined finishes to concentrate on delivering the most house at lower cost.

Embellishing simple forms is a dominant theme of America's popular architecture. In the case of the Foursquare and the Bungalow, Arts & Crafts or Colonial Revival influences were often seen. Queen Anne or Italian Villa touches enlivened many simple Homestead dwellings, often a generation or more after the "stylish" heyday of such ornament. Still, a good many of the houses have not a trace of ornament. In these cases, guessing construction dates may depend on knowing when the window size and shape they sport was popular, or when the materials with which they are built or faced came into use.

The Builder Style period was one of intense

innovation, with the development of new techniques and new materials, and vastly improved transportation facilities to deliver materials. For instance, from the 1870s onward, after the introduction of cast concrete, it was possible to build sturdy houses capable of giving a reasonable imitation of stone at only a fraction of the cost of stone. Stucco installed on top of wood or manmade sheathing was

---

A simple gable-front Homestead house of ca. 1910 in the Rosemont trolley-car suburb of Alexandria, Vir-

a new technique, and asbestos and asphalt shingles for roofs and siding was introduced. Although tile roofing was not a new material, it came into general use even on houses that were not Spanish in inspiration.

House Types

BASED ON THEIR FORM OR LAYOUT, WE HAVE SORTED Builder Style houses into four subcategories: Homestead, Foursquare, Bungalow, and cottage.

The simple Homestead house is generally tall, narrow, and deep, with a pitched roof and a gable front. It is sometimes called a "temple house" because the gable is often treated as a classical Greek pediment. The Homestead was well suited to narrow city or suburban lots; in fact, many of the city lots on which Homesteads stand today were suburban lots when these houses were built. It never entirely disappeared from the countryside after the 19th-century Greek Revival made it the farmhouse of preference. It is most often two storeys tall, but one- and one-and-a-half-storey versions are not uncommon, especially in the workmen's homes provided in company towns.

The Foursquare may be seen as a stripped-down version of late-18th- and mid-19th-century forms, including the Georgian block and the square Italianate house. The Foursquare was generally roomier than the Homestead; the plan might be seen as a sort of double Homestead. The roofline is pyramidal, or hipped, however, and not usually gabled. In its most elemental form, a Foursquare

This 1923 cottage in Washington, D.C., defines its type: small, low, and simple. It comes close to being a Bungalow but it lacks the Bungalow's low, sweeping roofline.

is simply four rooms on each of two floors, arranged one on each corner. It usually has a front porch, which may turn the corner on one side.

The simplest Foursquares have two single win-dows on the second floor, while more elegant houses may have two double or triple windows, or even a third set of windows. There may be a low small dormer with a flat or pyramidal roof. As the style becomes more elaborate, the dormer arrangement moves from one to two or three sash within each of the dormers, and in some houses there may be dormers on all four sides of the main roof.

Foursquares were most commonly built in

frame and stuccoed frame, but they are also found in stone and brick. "Shirtwaist" Foursquares typically have a belt course below the windows of the second floor, separating the different materials used on the first and second floors (stone below and stucco or clapboard above, for instance).

Most often built in frame or stucco over frame, cottages were only occasionally brick and even stone. Front porches are standard, but may not extend across the entire front of the building. Roofs are usually gabled as in the Bungalow, but they may take other forms as well. They may be

This Foursquare in River Forest, Illinois, shows the strong influence of the early-20th-century Prairie School, which flourished in the Chicago area.

very low, enclosing only a crawl space, or they may cover nearly an entire floor. There may or may not be dormers. Porte cochères are rarely found. The plan may be rectangular or L-shaped, always with an informal and picturesque effect. When there is ornament, it may be in the style of Queen Anne houses. Windows are varied, tending to be more vertical than horizontal.

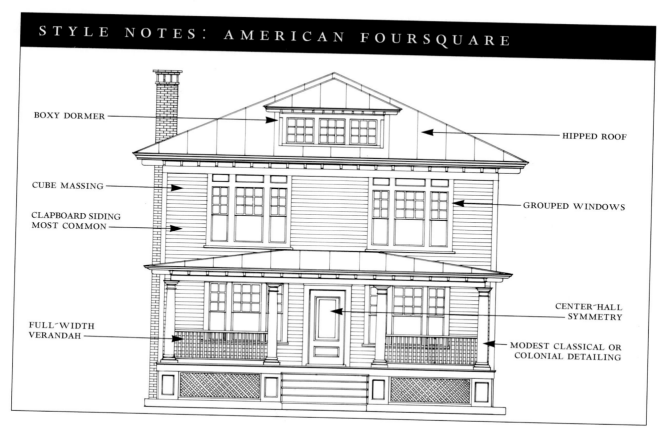

STYLE NOTES: AMERICAN FOURSQUARE

BOXY DORMER

HIPPED ROOF

CUBE MASSING

GROUPED WINDOWS

CLAPBOARD SIDING MOST COMMON

CENTER-HALL SYMMETRY

FULL-WIDTH VERANDAH

MODEST CLASSICAL OR COLONIAL DETAILING

ROMANTIC REVIVALS

[1890-1940]

O F ALL THE PICTURESQUE, INFORMAL STYLES THAT PIQUED AMERICAN HOMEBUILDERS' IMAGI-nations in the first third of the 20th century, the most popular ones were those rooted in English traditions. Besides the ever-dominant American colonial and Georgian styles (which were, of course, mostly British themselves), homeowners on this side of the Atlantic could choose from a broad range of English Revival architecture based on medieval, Gothic, or Tudor traditions of the 15th through 17th centuries. Their houses bespoke old-fashioned coziness (the cottage), dignified prosperity (the manor house), or even ancient nobility (the castle), while keeping the solid comfort of 20th-century amenities. ▪ After World War I, America was engaged in a burst of suburban building, as families in un-precedented numbers bought and built their own homes. With so many new builders and buyers, some were bound to want something different. The war had sparked an interest

At Meadowbrook Hall in Birmingham, Michigan (1927–29), complex chimneys, decorated vergeboard, and aged timbers suggest another era altogether. Smith, Hinchman, and Grylls, architects.

among Americans in English and European buildings. At the same time there was easier access to foreign ideas through books, travel, and even movies.

In traditional English houses additions and changes by successive generations produced rambling layouts, and a seemingly unplanned informality. Cottages and even large manor houses were often "half-timbered," i.e., heavy wooden framing members were filled in with "nogging" of brick or wattle and daub, a combination of small wood sticks and mud plaster. The term "Elizabethan" has sometimes been used as a blanket term for all half-timbered buildings, but the practice was common in other periods. Tudor is the term often used to describe Old English masonry

houses, usually brick. The Tudor arch was a hallmark of the period. Other features included Flemish gables (shaped, curved gables based on those seen in Holland), massive chimney stacks with multiple flues, second-floor overhangs, wide wooden vergeboards with decorative carving, and casement windows with small glass panes set in leaded mullions of diamond or lattice design. Bay windows and oriels were commonly used to light the dark interiors. Heavy paneled wood doors were common.

But in 20th-century houses that imitated these early buildings, ground-hugging designs based on cottages created a cozy, homelike effect. These were often carefully designed to look as if they had been built of brick or stone even though it was likely that their masonry veneers were applied over a modern wood frame. Cement-based stucco was also often applied directly over frame construction, and exposed timbers were likely to be only surface decoration. Stucco was sometimes "weathered" to make it appear as if portions had fallen off the wall, exposing the timbers and nog-

ging beneath. Timbers were adzed and stained or even charred to simulate old woodwork.

Visual interest came from textured surfaces and a mixture of several different facing materials: brick with stone trim at doorways, window surrounds, and building corners; plaster (stucco) and wood; and, sometimes, ornamental cast-plaster panels or parging. The picturesque effect of brick walls was sometimes enhanced by laying unevenly sized bricks in a staggered pattern that mixed dark irregular "clinker" bricks with regular ones. Gable-roofed, one-room wings were perfect for entrances or living rooms and lent a picturesque air to the facade, while side-swept *catslide* roofs over entries were nearly a cliché. Shingle, tile, or composition roofs were laid in irregular patterns and varying colors to suggest thatching. Irregular, projecting chimneys of stone or brick, with

Among the most picturesque features of the English style are imitations of thatched roofs, and the irregular line between stucco and stonework, suggesting that the stucco has fallen off from age, thus exposing the stonework. This example from the 1920s is in the Wesley Heights section of Washington, D.C.

This 1929 Old English house in Scarsdale, New York, features partial half-timbering with a small oriel window, and a steep gable roof with unusually large and irregular slates.

chimney pots and multiple stacks, were useful as well as picturesque, so almost every house had one, often on a front wall.

For larger, high-style houses, a good architect might come up with something that hardly could be distinguished from a real castle or manor house. Architects often made their reputations with artfully designed, "archeologically correct" suburban or country homes for wealthy clients. The best American architects used the English styles as a springboard to their own creative reinterpretations, to the enhancement of areas such as Philadelphia's English Village in Chestnut Hill and other early-20th-century trolley and railroad suburbs.

The English cottage style was prominently

featured in ready-cut house and plan catalogs, where it was highly regarded for its picturesque facades. Interior layouts were strictly 20th-century creations, however; the plans not only fit modern convenience into a medieval-looking house, they also tied interiors to gardens and yards. French doors and large windows were liberally used. Nearly every house had a breakfast nook off the kitchen, testament to the fact that almost all the housework was by then being done by the housewife (aided by better kitchen planning and more electrical appliances).

To offset this modern floor plan, the decorative scheme for the Old English house aimed for a weighty medieval style with Renaissance overtones. It might start with oak wall paneling stained dark brown and extending from floor to ceiling, a bit of carved linenfold paneling, and recessed cupboards set into the wall. Then there had to be a fireplace (or, better yet, several) of stone or terra cotta with elaborate carved jambs, lintels, and ceiling-high overmantels. Libraries had considerable cachet, even in small houses, and bookshelves were heavy and substantial. Recessed windowseats

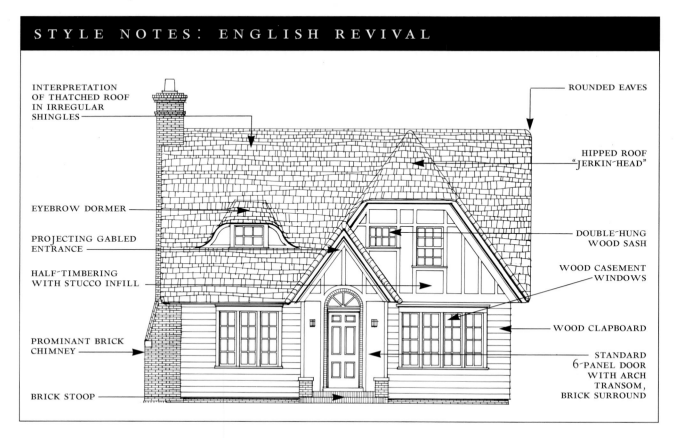

STYLE NOTES: ENGLISH REVIVAL

INTERPRETATION OF THATCHED ROOF IN IRREGULAR SHINGLES

ROUNDED EAVES

HIPPED ROOF "JERKIN-HEAD"

EYEBROW DORMER

PROJECTING GABLED ENTRANCE

HALF-TIMBERING WITH STUCCO INFILL

DOUBLE-HUNG WOOD SASH

WOOD CASEMENT WINDOWS

WOOD CLAPBOARD

PROMINENT BRICK CHIMNEY

STANDARD 6-PANEL DOOR WITH ARCH TRANSOM, BRICK SURROUND

BRICK STOOP

The eyebrow dormers, Flemish gables, massive chimneys and masonry walls of this Washington, D.C., residence of ca. 1920 were common ingredients of the English Romantic Revival style.

took advantage of bay windows and oriels. As for floors, the best were of stone. Plain wide boards or parquetry in herringbone, checkered, or geometrical patterns gave a nice effect, or linoleum in an imitative pattern could fake it. Beamed ceilings with thick, dark, wooden or plaster beams finished to look like wood, and sand-finished plaster or or-

namental parge-work panels capped things off. Ornamental plaster in Old English designs, even the beams themselves, could be purchased by the foot from ornamental-plaster companies.

As family life turned toward backyard patios and basement recreation rooms, and as the automobile age dawned, there was at least one architectural casualty—the front porch. Long the hub of social life, it died quietly, a victim of disinterest. But if one space was lost, another was gained: the garage. By the 1920s, the automobile had become almost a member of the family, one that

needed a room of its own, usually in a freestanding garage in the corner of the yard, but sometimes in one attached to the house.

The Mary Stewart house exemplifies the elegant, formal French-style house. This is in the Kalorama section of Washington, D.C., and was designed by Paul Cret in 1938.

French Revivals

THE FIRST WAVE OF FRENCH INFLUENCE IN AMERICA was a regional phenomenon, occurring when 17th- and 18th-century French settlers built raised cottages along the Gulf Coast and up the Missis- sippi River. The second wave was a design influence begun just before the Civil War, signaled by the mansard roofs of the Second Empire style, that affected the entire country by the 1870s. A third wave crested in the turn-of-the-century Beaux Arts school of Academic Classicism, and created reproductions of formal French Renaissance country châteaux and city houses.

Then, from about 1915 until about 1940, a romanticized, informal French style blossomed, based more on the farmhouse, especially those of Normandy, than on the mansion. It played a small but significant role in the history of 20th-century Revival architecture, which continued to be dominated by Georgian and Spanish traditions. After

The round entrance tower and conical roof of this 1920s house in Summit, New Jersey, mark this as French Revival, reinterpreting the traditional Norman farmhouse or small manor.

World War I, buildings in the new French style could be found all across the continent, whereas Spanish and Mediterranean houses found their largest audience in the South and West. French-style houses were few, but they might turn up anywhere, even in California or Florida.

Unlike Spanish-style *casas*, however, they did not necessarily show up in the places most expected. New Orleans, with its vibrant French heritage, had to wait until the 1960s for a new French building fashion. Mostly, the French building boomlet of the 1920s and 1930s occurred in suburban areas of large eastern and midwestern cities with, of course, a detour to southern California, where the style took on Hollywood airs.

There are two informal groups of French Re-

vival houses: the first, the Norman farmhouse or small manor; the second, an American eclectic style that draws heavily on the image of French farmhouses. Many houses of picturesque and evocative design were built in well-to-do eastern suburbs of Philadelphia, New York, Chicago, and other large cities. At the other end of the eclectic scale are the freely interpreted and often charming little houses that were picked up by house-plan and ready-cut-house distributors and local builders all across the nation.

French houses are generally built of masonry

with steep pyramidal or hipped roofs. Mansard roofs are also found, as are, less frequently, high gable roofs. Round or polygonal towers with curved roofs were common, especially at the entrance.

A lingering question pesters old-house observers: English or French? Tudor or Norman? It can be devilishly hard to tell the difference between

This 1920s interpretation of the Norman farmhouse is in West Chester, Pennsylvania, a good example of the fine Philadelphia suburban houses of this period.

In Cape May, New Jersey, The Villa (1905) is a good Mission-style house with sloped gables, picture window, and pergola.

houses supposedly based on English cottages of the Middle Ages and those based on French farmhouses of the same period. As a very general rule, "French" houses are more likely to have arched doors and windows, wrought-iron balconies, and conical roof towers. Steeply pitched *catslide* roofs graced many entrances and bays of small 1920s and '30s houses. Both "English" and "Norman" examples are really an American Romantic style, merging features of both types—especially in suburbs around major cities.

Prior to World War II, the French Revival succumbed to competition from the Colonial Revival and other Revival styles, particularly the vigorous Spanish and Mediterranean. The post-war emergence of new house forms, such as the ranch-house and the split-level, also did not immediately suggest ways to incorporate French styling. By the 1960s, however, the French romantic style would re-emerge with a fresh vitality.

Mediterranean Styles

DURING THE EARLY 20TH CENTURY, MOST AMERICANS settled into well-equipped modern houses built in Colonial Revival styles that celebrated the English roots of our founding fathers. But in California, Florida, and the Southwest —where the past was not English but Spanish— the term "colonial revival" took on a different meaning and an entirely different look. Spanish-influenced buildings had a double charm, for they not only bespoke an important era in American history, but also conjured

At El Jardin in Coconut Grove, Florida, Spanish Churrigueresque ornament embellishes the entry. This fine Mediterranean house was designed by Kiennel and Elliott in 1917.

up romantic images of far-away, long-ago European countrysides. Three of the architectural sub-styles that evolved from this Hispanic heritage—Mission, Spanish Colonial Revival, and Mediterranean— spread across the country in the years between 1890 and World War II. Despite their foreign ancestry, all these styles are unmistakably American. The Spanish and Mediterranean (which was Spanish plus Italian plus French) styles worked well for houses of every size, as well as for other building types, from city halls to hotels, motels, and service stations. Although the Mediterranean styles were seen throughout the United States, they flourished in warm climates, particularly California, southern Florida, and the Southwest.

Linking all these styles was the play of sunlight and shadow on thick, stuccoed walls and across tiled roofs. The stucco finish common to nearly every building in every Spanish or Mediterranean style lent an impression of solidity. Once in a great while, there was a brick example without stucco or, even more rarely, a clapboarded house with a patio. The stucco could be smooth and white as plaster or roughly textured like that of a Spanish farmhouse. Sometimes it was applied in thin layers until it achieved an undulating effect that suggested annual applications over many years. The exterior colors were mostly sunshine hues and warm earth tones: white or ochres, pale pinks, yellows, and grays.

Round-arched doorways and windows were protected by wrought-iron grilles and balconies and shielded from glaring sunlight and the gaze of curious passersby by striped awnings mounted on spearlike struts. Since the age was as enamored of technology as of history, casement windows of wood or, more often, steel, were usual. Red tile roofs typified all the Spanish and Mediterranean styles. They were usually low-pitched, hipped, or with very low gables. Sometimes a false gable front hid a flat roof behind. While barrel or "S"

The exotic Vizcaya mansion of 1916 in Miami, Florida, designed by Pauk Chalfin and F. Burral Hoffman, Jr., is Italian in its derivation, and fits the Mediterranean label neatly.

tiles were standard, shingles were sometimes used. Chimneys were not usually prominent.

The first and most important of the Spanish styles to be picked up by the revivalists was the Mission Style (sometimes called the Mission Revival), loosely based on the adobe churches built by Spanish priests during the early settlement period. Interest in the missions was reawakened in the 1890s by influential writers bent not just on saving them, but also on encouraging the development of the Mission Style. Faced with a flood of early-20th-century immigrants from eastern states, California looked to its Spanish and Indian past for inspiration in designing new homes. The missions provided an attractive, adaptable precedent.

Simplicity was the hallmark of the Mission Style. Thick, white stucco walls pierced by unframed round-arch openings and low-pitched tile roofs were ubiquitous. Rooflines frequently ended in shaped or parapeted gables, often decorated with cartouches and quatrefoil windows. Arcades and recessed porches suggested the quiet, shaded walks of Franciscan monasteries. Arches were supported by simple piers or columns, or they sprang directly from the base of the walls. Domes and "bell towers" added picturesque interest.

The union of Spanish Colonial Revival and Mission Style took place in 1915. The Panama-California Exposition in San Diego highlighted spectacular Mexican-Baroque buildings by Bertram Grosvenor Goodhue and other distinguished architects. By the 1920s, Spanish Colonial Revival architecture had overcome every competing style in California, and examples were showing up all across the nation.

Like Mission Style buildings, those in the Spanish Colonial Revival style have stucco walls, tile roofs, and, often, arched openings. Unlike the Mission Style buildings, Spanish Colonial Revival houses sometimes displayed dazzling ornament. Irregular, picturesque building outlines en-

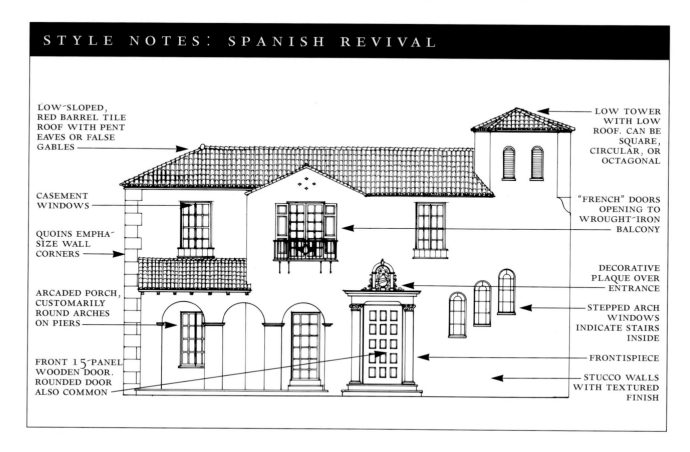

STYLE NOTES: SPANISH REVIVAL

LOW-SLOPED, RED BARREL TILE ROOF WITH PENT EAVES OR FALSE GABLES

CASEMENT WINDOWS

QUOINS EMPHA-SIZE WALL CORNERS

ARCADED PORCH, CUSTOMARILY ROUND ARCHES ON PIERS

FRONT 15-PANEL WOODEN DOOR. ROUNDED DOOR ALSO COMMON

LOW TOWER WITH LOW ROOF. CAN BE SQUARE, CIRCULAR, OR OCTAGONAL

"FRENCH" DOORS OPENING TO WROUGHT-IRON BALCONY

DECORATIVE PLAQUE OVER ENTRANCE

STEPPED ARCH WINDOWS INDICATE STAIRS INSIDE

FRONTISPIECE

STUCCO WALLS WITH TEXTURED FINISH

In Los Angeles, California, this fully developed Spanish Colonial Revival house of c. 1925 features the typical arched picture window, low rounded entrance tower, and a small octagonal tower, as well as a driveway arch.

livened flat walls. Low round or octagonal towers with low-pitched tiled roofs were common, sometimes placed at the intersection of two wings. Applied ornament, particularly the flamboyant Churrigueresque (Spanish Baroque) or Plateresque (16th-century Spanish/Moorish) types were popular on high-style examples. Entrance doors were usually large and high, and made of heavy wood, either carved, paneled, or nail-studded. Windows were not usually symmetrically placed. Although generally small, they were not uniform in size, even in the same facade.

An exception to the small-window rule is a large, round-arch window frequently found in the end of a projecting gable-roofed wing. Patios are less typical in this style than in the Mission Style. However, pergolas are very popular. Balconies and decorative *rejas*, or window grilles, of wrought-iron or with turned wooden spindles were common, and the spindles were often painted in lively colors.

The Spanish-Italian-American hybrid known in the United States as "Mediterranean" style was like nothing seen in any Mediterranean land. This umbrella term reflects the diverse European building traditions that inspired the movement: primarily Spanish with Moorish tendencies and Italian, with an occasional touch of French. Structures with the strongest remembrance to those of Spain and Mexico were likely to be labeled Spanish Colonial Revival, while the term Italian was applied to the most formal and symmetrical buildings in the 1920s and 1930s. The term "Mediterranean" was later used for large stylish houses that suggest no

A symmetrical facade, formal entryway, arched windows, and Spanish tiles distinguish this house of ca. 1920 in Pensacola, Florida.

Ceramic wall tiles in geometric Moorish patterns or figural tiles were popular for dadoes and on fireplace surrounds. Arched openings connected living areas, and small wall niches provided a place to display interesting objects. Wrought-iron grilles, stair rails, wall sconces, chandeliers, and hardware were essential to the Mediterranean ambiance.

Pueblo Revival

NO AMERICAN ARCHITECTURAL STYLE IS MORE CLOSELY tied to a single region than the simple, blocky, adobe pueblo. In the Southwest, and particularly in New Mexico and Arizona, the pueblo looks as natural as the strong yellow sunlight and red clay soil that give the land and buildings their color. Once the pueblo magic had been translated into waterproof, 20th-century building materials, however, there was nothing to stop its being built in eastern, midwestern, or Pacific coastal areas.

specific place or country, but reinterpret ideas from several. This eclectic approach provided a place for symmetry and classical ornament, although these are far from universal in Mediterranean-style houses.

Mediterranean- and Spanish-style houses had patio-like features, although few had true patios enclosed on all sides by roofed living areas. These sheltered outdoor "rooms" were extremely useful in a period of shrinking indoor spaces. Recessed porches at entrances gave shadowy relief from the stark wall surfaces.

Inside the house, tile floors, waxed to suggest age, and wide oak boards were favored. For the budget-conscious, linoleum and composition tile flooring were satisfactory substitutes. Walls were plain, often rough-plastered, and tinted or painted in a light or neutral tones. Beamed ceilings of dark, weathered-looking wood was a rare use of wood trim in Spanish houses, and rich, vivid colors were encouraged in fabrics to complement the neutral walls.

The first phase of the Pueblo style was embodied by the indigenous dwellings of the Pueblo Indians, a building type already well developed when the Spaniards came. It survives, barely changed, today. The second phase came when Spanish settlers added their knowledge of design and building techniques to what the Native Americans were doing. The third, or Territorial, phase marked the arrival of Anglo settlers who introduced double-hung wood windows and machine-made millwork. The fourth phase was a revival that began in the wake of the early-20th-century railroad-tourist expansion into the Southwest, and was fed by the contemporaneous Arts & Crafts Movement's emphasis on natural materials and forms. This revival reinterpreted both Pueblo and Territorial buildings.

Native pueblo forms were visually appealing in their simplicity and built for security. Constructed of mud-plastered adobe, strung together like stacks of gently eroded, matte-finished sugar cubes, pueblos had slightly rounded corners, battered walls, and set-back second and third storeys. Entrance was by ladders to the roof; from there the occupant descended into the interior. There were no real windows, but only occasional small openings. The roofs were supported by rounded

A typical small Pueblo Revival house of ca. 1925 in Santa Fe, New Mexico, picturesquely rendered in warm stucco with a corner porch replete with projecting vigas.

logs called *vigas* that projected at the ends. These were covered with saplings, or *latillas*, and twigs or straw, and packed with earth as the final covering. The Spanish organized their adobe houses around a central patio, with access through a passageway, called a *zaguan*, and added ornament and classically derived details, especially in churches.

These early designs were revived at the beginning of the 20th century, and flourished in the 1920s and '30s with reinterpretations of the original pueblo adobe houses and the 19th-century Territorial house. They were generally stuccoed in earth tones to simulate adobe. They featured projecting *vigas*, covered porches, or *portales*, and steel casement windows more often than double-hung wood sash. Although they are represented in many parts of the country, most Pueblo Revival houses are found in the Southwest.

MODERN STYLES

[1920-1950]

A MID THE WELTER OF NOSTALGIC STYLES that kept architects busy recreating the past in the early 20th century, it was inevitable that some people would be itching to get on with the present—and, even better, the future. Two architectural trends came out of the renewed interest in looking ahead rather than backward: the Art Deco or Moderne Style and the International Style. In part, both styles were European developments that took on new dimensions when they crossed the Atlantic. Neither style could challenge the entrenched claims of the Colonial Revival on the affection of American home-builders, however, and so their immediate effect on housing was limited. The less important of the two styles, Art Deco, began to peter out around 1940, although buildings with Moderne features continued to be built into the early 1950s. The International Style, so

---

Frank Lloyd Wright's work is best regarded as Modern; it was neither International Style nor Art Deco, although in his masterwork, Fallingwater, at Bear Run, Pennsylvania, 1937, he leans heavily toward the International Style, using concrete planes projecting at angles to each other over a waterfall.

This 1930s Pensacola, Florida, house has a typical Art Deco entry and door with curved concrete canopy and fluted columns.

called because it had roots in several European countries—particularly Germany, Austria, Holland, and France—merged into the Modern Movement, which became widely accepted after World War II. Important American architects laid the groundwork for the blossoming of the modern trend on this side of the Atlantic, among them Frank Lloyd Wright, Irving J. Gill, and George Howe. Although he refused to endorse the International Style and ignored Art Deco, Wright actually provided the initial inspiration for much of the European interest in Modernism. Gill used Ameri-

can themes to produce designs with a distinctly International flavor.

Nevertheless, the strongest impetus for both the Art Deco and the International styles came from the European, not the American, architectural community. Wright, the individualist, continued to work in his own distinctive idiom, creating a new modern style in southern California and Arizona in the 1920s and 1930s, and following with his Usonian houses of the later 1930s.

Art Deco

THE CRITICAL THRUST FOR ART DECO CAME FROM THE Exposition des Arts Décoratifs et Industriels Modernes in Paris in 1925. There were two facets of the Art Deco style: Zigzag and Streamlined. Zigzag was largely a system of low-relief, angular ornament applied to smooth building surfaces, and was popular from around the end of World War I until about 1930. Then it was overtaken by Streamlined (sometimes called Moderne), which abandoned ornament almost entirely in order to focus on streamlined forms such as smooth walls, rounded

edges, and circular windows. Both made extensive use of steel casement windows.

Zigzag Art Deco pulled its motifs from various sources, including Native American design. The repertoire included chevrons, circles, and stepped-back lines with strong vertical accents.

In architecture, the flashy Zigzag style put a modern spin on traditionally designed buildings. Skyscrapers, commercial buildings, and large apartment buildings stood to benefit more from the

---

This 1937 house in Albuquerque, New Mexico, is a model of its type: Streamlined Moderne, with a striking two-storey rounded corner filled with glass blocks.

Architect Joseph Goddeyne's own house of ca. 1939 in Bay City, Michigan, is a blend of Art Deco with some International Style. The rounded bay built with glass blocks is notable, as is its construction from precast, asbestos-cement panels.

Zigzag style than houses, so it flourished mostly in big cities (particularly New York and Los Angeles) where Deco skyscrapers added zest to the urban skyline. In low-rise models, Zigzag Deco appeared in California and Florida for hotels and apartment buildings, as well as commercial and public buildings. Zigzag decorative elements sometimes made their way onto house facades of the 1920s and 1930s. Floor plans and construction techniques were pretty much the same as in buildings constructed in other styles of the period. Flat roofs, stuccoed walls, extensive areas of glass blocks, and strips of steel casement windows established the Deco-style credentials. Windows and doors were set flush with the wall surface, with no sills or lintels to interrupt the flow of flat walls. Striking vertical elements, stepped-back walls, cut-out building corners, or windows that wrapped around the corner of the building enlivened stark, crisply angled silhouettes. Small circular windows and slightly raised or incised ornament, sometimes in polychromed terra cotta, were often used to provide color and interest.

Moderne or Streamlined Deco was well suited to industrial design, from automobiles and airplanes to toasters and coffeepots. Streamlined designs implied speed and efficiency, so it was not surprising that transportation became Moderne's special theme. Airports and bus stations, as well as airplanes and buses, were built to its specifications. The Streamlined approach also had a persuasive logic viewed from the perspective of Depression-era economics. Whereas Zigzag Deco's success depended largely on fine materials, artistically wrought and skillfully applied (i.e., expensive), the stripped-down Streamlined forms—typified in architecture by horizontal bands of windows and rounded corners—often were its only ornament. The simplicity of the Streamlined style makes it easy to distinguish from the Zigzag; its smooth edges set it apart from both the Zigzag and the International Style that developed at the same time. In Streamlined buildings, the emphasis was unflinchingly horizontal, an effect reinforced by bands of steel windows, incised string courses, and flat roofs. Streamlined walls usually ended in curves.

Richard Neutra's Lovell House in Los Angeles, California, was built in 1929 in a striking International Style design on a steep hillside. It is one of the most important early works in the new style in the United States.

International Style

ART DECO HAS RECENTLY COME BACK INTO FAVOR. THE International Style, however, was by far the more important of the two phenomena in an architectural sense, and professional architects had it firmly in hand from the beginning. The International Style started in Europe, although there were key developments, such as the skyscraper and the Prairie School house, taking place in America. The new style was a response to the opportunities supplied by modern technology. It was also a rebellion against what Modernists saw as the messy eclecticism of the late-19th and early-20th

centuries. The International Style seemed uniquely suited to the Machine Age. It was clean-lined, completely functional, and rigorously geometric. Here was a style, its proponents believed, that could be used for any building in any price range at any level of architectural sophistication from banks to workingmen's houses. There was no need to grope about in a stylistic grab bag for the best form for a particular kind of building. Like the earlier Arts & Crafts Movement, the International Style was as much a crusade that espoused social and philosophical ideas about morality and the pursuit of human happiness as it was about architecture.

Not everybody liked it. Most Americans

found the new building style ugly, and preferred to stick with traditional forms and Beaux Arts ideals. Still, American architects such as Irving J. Gill had been experimenting for many years with pared-down architectural forms based on Spanish Mission designs in buildings constructed of modern concrete and steel. And, despite his expressed distaste for the style, Frank Lloyd Wright himself produced several houses in a modified International style, including Fallingwater, an internationally famous residence.

Other architects working in America had been exposed to modern architecture through their European schooling. Since 1914 a Viennese advocate of Internationalism, Rudolph Schindler, had been in the United States, working for a time in Wright's office. Richard Neutra, a classmate of Schindler, came from Vienna in 1919. By 1926 the two were practicing architecture together in southern California, an area that proved to be particularly receptive to Modernism.

Just before World War II, the International Style achieved a solid foothold in the United States. Walter Gropius, a German refugee from Nazism, is probably the most important contributor to America's International Style movement. Gropius had organized the Bauhaus, a German academy for avant-garde artists, architects, and designers. He fled Germany in 1934; his Hungarian colleague at the Bauhaus, Marcel Breuer, left in 1937. Both men wound up on the architectural faculty at Harvard University in 1937. Shortly thereafter, Gropius's successor as director of the Bauhaus, Mies van der

The Walter Bixby House in Kansas City, Missouri, was designed by architect Edward W. Tanner in 1935. Long and low, it combines the smooth walls of Art Deco with the more rigorous abstract geometry of the International Style.

Rohe, also emigrated to the United States, to direct what is now the architecture department at the Illinois Institute of Technology in Chicago.

With these influential thinkers established in architectural schools and offices around the nation, a generation of American architects began to move out of the realm of the Beaux Arts and into the modern design arena.

Gropius's design for his home in Lincoln, Massachusetts, tells much about the International Style as it developed in the United States. There are characteristically flat walls, flat roofs, bands of windows, and a total lack of ornament. Even though the house looks deceptively like a simple rectangle, its projecting and receding walls and roofs "express" the spaces within. No wall, window, or roofline obeys any arbitrary architectural rule. Instead of the outer walls dictating where rooms can be placed, the spaces inside the house determine where the outer walls will go. (This is somewhat like the difference between packing an object into a box and shrinkwrapping it.) Every part of the design has a function. Should it bring a lovely view within reach of those who live in the house? Should it shelter them from a hot summer sun without depriving them of solar heat in the winter? Gropius's house gives us a picture of the architect as problem-solver.

International Style architects assumed that their buildings would use the most up-to-date technology and modern materials—steel, concrete, plastic, and glass panes of almost infinite size that were to be honestly expressed in the design. Ac-

Architect Walter Gropius's own house in Lincoln, Massachusetts, built in 1937-8, exemplifies the rigorous geometry and functional design of the International Style.

tually, however, such materials were not cheap, and neither was the technology required to build with them. Steel and concrete frames worked well for big commercial and public buildings, but few homeowners could afford them. Thus, many houses of the International Style are based on a wood fram-ing system with stucco or on concrete-block or hol-low-tile construction. Gropius's house, for in-stance, is of wood with vertical wood siding.

The roofline of International Style houses is virtually always flat. While there may be fire-places and large chimneys, the chimneys are treated

quietly as just one more expressive projection. Windows are usually large and always rectangular. Window walls are common. Clerestory windows located just below the ceiling line, wraparound corner windows, and sliding-glass doors are standard features.

The floor plans of International Style houses acknowledged that life in the 20th century was changing. There was less formality, and there was certainly a lot less household help. Consequently, there are fewer maids' rooms and isolated work areas such as separate kitchens and laundries. In fact, except for bedrooms, bathrooms, and sometimes kitchens, these open plans usually offer not individual rooms so much as interactive spaces, which may be inside, outside, or, with the help of sliding doors or screens, a little or a lot of both.

Philip Johnson's Glass House in New Canaan, Connecticut, was built by the architect as his own residence. Although not built until 1949, it epitomizes the International Style image of steel and glass set in a rigid form with a fully open plan, something few homeowners would be comfortable with. Opposite: Wright's Pope-Leighey House is a 1939 Usonian model at Mount Vernon, Virginia.

POSTSCRIPT: POSTWAR HOUSES

WORLD WAR II WAS behind them, and America's fighting men and women had come home to government-insured mortgages, a robust postwar economy, and small families that were about to get bigger. Home ownership beckoned. But homes had to be built before they could be bought. And what would the new houses of the late 1940s and 1950s be like? Mingled with the Cape Cods and Colonial Revivals left over from prewar days were less familiar house types—ranch houses, split-levels, and even prefabs.

Okay, we hear you. *That's* not historical architecture, you're protesting. That's the house you grew up in—the one with the basement rec room, an American car in the carport, and Mom in the kitchen putting Redi-Wip on the cherry Jell-O. We know. But that house and others like it are

now headed for their 50th birthdays, when they will become potentially eligible for listing on the National Register of Historic Places. And the truth is, they really don't build houses like that anymore.

The pent-up yearning for a house with a yard that hit the parents of baby-boomers came out of a four-year war with strict rationing of building materials and labor, which had been preceded by twelve years of nationwide economic hardship— sixteen years of building postponed. A lot of houses were needed. Government estimates at the end of the war projected a demand for 12.5 million new housing units by 1955.

Surging costs for labor and materials after the war meant that most houses would be small, but there was plenty of relatively cheap land in buildable but remote locations. Miles beyond the borders of major cities and industrial areas, developers bought up thousands of acres of farmland and began constructing whole towns of little houses, using assembly-line methods to reduce the need for skilled craftsmen. These cookie-cutter developments stirred indignation among architects and

This Morristown, New Jersey, house combines the characteristics of two dominant house types of the postwar period—the split-level and the ranch house, which are artfully expressed in its horizontal lines and three-bay front porch.

intellectuals, but not among the people who lived in them. Between 1947 and 1952, Levitt and Sons, the most famous developer of the era, constructed more than 17,000 fully equipped houses in Long Island potato fields. Since most of these new centerless towns were accessible only by car, they helped make the automotive industry the great multiplier factor of America's peacetime economy.

Throughout the postwar era, architects designed modern boxes with flat or butterfly roofs, clerestory windows, and cantilevered rooms. For the mass market, however, the most innovative residence types were the ranch house and the split-level, both designed to eke out maximum living space from the least square footage. Both house types exploited the trend toward horizontal living on wide building lots, as their shallow profiles made the most of available light and views.

The wide, low lines of this house in Virginia Beach, Virginia, mark the move away from the colonial traditions to the ranch house. This example features a hipped roof recalling both eastern U.S. traditions, as well as the midwestern Prairie house.

The ranch house was a loose adaptation of a one-storey house with a long, ground-level front porch, which was popularly assumed to be typical of ranch dwellings in the American west. The split-level offered a single storey at one end and two storeys at the other, with the entrance on a level somewhere in between the two storeys. In both the ranch and the split-level, the basic modernism of the house was sometimes softened by "traditional" decorative effects, such as a couple of narrow stationary shutters at a picture window or a black

This is the distinctive split-level house developed during the postwar era, with the living room on grade at the left, a sunken garage to the right, and bedrooms upstairs. It is in Chatham, New Jersey.

aluminum eagle above the front door.

The automobile became a *de facto* family member with the move to the suburbs, taking up a place of honor at the front of the house in either a carport or an attached two-car garage. Indeed, the carport, a descendant of the more stately *porte cochère*, was among the most typical features of the postwar house. This versatile space served a multitude of purposes: toddler's play yard, outdoor kitchen for the charcoal grill, and storage area.

Construction methods and materials also underwent a profound change. The prefabricated house, and particularly the prefabricated metal house, had been heralded as the wave of the future by architectural pundits during the Depression and war years. The most famous postwar name in the prefab metal

housing industry was Lustron, which manufactured an all-steel house that sold for $9,000. All interior and exterior surfaces, except for the aluminum window frames, were of porcelainized steel. Although Lustron and other metal-house manufacturers were unable to make their ventures profitable and eventually went out of business, their innovative approach had a lasting impact on the housing industry. From mobile homes to suburban tract houses, the American postwar home satisfied a craving for comfort, convenience, and familiarity enclosed in a traditional building envelope with up-to-the-minute materials, kitchens, bathrooms, heating and cooling systems, insulation, siding, roofing, and windows.

WHERE WILL AMERICAN HOUSE STYLES GO NOW? AMERican houses, as we have seen, have most often been American amalgams—adaptations based on European history or our own, tempered by the demands of contemporary living and the promises of contemporary technology. Future design sources may well be found in the amazing range of styles chronicled in this book. They are already apparent in the interest in *new* revival styles: Queen Anne houses, Arts & Crafts bungalows, Norman farmhouses, Italian villas, English half-timbered manor houses, and neoclassical "mansions" with a column or two to suggest a portico, and updated versions of the Cape Cod cottage and other variations on the colonial theme, often with a pronounced regional twist. What could possibly be next? How about a contemporary revival of the International Style?

Glossary

ADOBE Sun-dried earth, generally with a straw binder, often shaped into bricks by hand or in forms, or used directly as a mortar or "plaster" finish.

ARCADE A row of arched openings as in a porch or patio.

ARCH HEAD A round-arch top to a doorway or window.

ASHLAR Stonework of square or rectangular stones, usually laid in a regular pattern and, unless otherwise qualified, has a smooth-tooled finish.

BALLOON FRAME Light timber framing using studs (commonly 2" x 4") closely spaced; developed in the U.S. in the 1830s.

BALUSTER A short post or column supporting the railing of a stair or balustrade.

BALUSTRADE A railing or parapet with balusters and railing, with or without a base.

BARGEBOARD, OR VERGEBOARD Face board, often decorated, on the eaves edge of a gable roof.

BATTERED A term used to describe a wall or pier that slopes gently inward as it rises.

BATTLEMENT In medieval (and revival) architecture, a rooftop parapet penetrated by slots, originally for archers, later for ornament.

BAY The basic descriptive term for the exterior breadth of a building, measured by the number of openings for doors and windows or other dividing features, as in a "four-bay facade."

BAY WINDOW A multipart window that projects from the wall surface, usually with angled windows at the sides, extending from the ground up one or more storeys; if curved, it becomes a bow window (See also Oriel).

BELT COURSE, OR STRING COURSE A slightly projecting plain or molded band across a facade, usually between floor levels.

BELVEDERE Generally, an open pavilion on the roof of a building.

BOARD-AND-BATTEN 19th-century frame construction of vertical boards, with their joints covered by narrow wood strips (battens).

BOX CORNICE Plain, undecorated cornice comprised of a horizontal bottom and a vertical front board, without moldings or enrichments.

BRACKET A large structural member, often ornamented, supporting projecting parts of a building, such as a roof's eaves or oriel. Most often it is a three-piece triangular work, though it may contain decorative elements within the triangle, or even be a solid member or an inverted L-shape.

BROWNSTONE A brown sandstone; the most distinctive is a dark, reddish-brown stone from New Jersey and Connecticut. Row houses with brownstone ashlar facades are sometimes called "brownstones."

CAMPANILE Correctly, a bell tower, sometimes applied to a tower on a house if tall and small in plan.

CAPITAL In classical architecture, the decorated or molded top part of a column, pier, or pilaster.

CARTOUCHE An ornamental panel, traditionally in the form of a scroll of paper, with an inscription or date and set in a frame.

CASEMENT A window hinged to swing outward.

CASTELLATED In Gothic Revival architecture, resembling a fortified castle with turrets and battlements.

CATSLIDE In early American architecture, the steeply sloped roofline of an addition to the rear of a house, continuing the main roofline back and down low, forming a house known as a saltbox.

CAVETTO A large, concave curved molding, often used in cornices.

CENTER-HALL PLAN A house type with a central hall running front to back, with rooms on each side of the hall.

CENTRAL, OR MAIN, BLOCK The principal and central part of a house that has wings or flanking pavilions.

CENTRAL COURT An open court-yard within the block of a large house; a patio (Spanish).

CHAMFER An angled cut along the edge of a post or beam.

CHIMNEY POT An extension of a chimney flue above the chimney itself, usually decorated and com-monly made of brick or terra-cotta, but sometimes of cast iron.

COFFER A recessed panel in a flat or vaulted ceiling.

COLONNETTE A short or small column, often used for a decorative purpose.

COLONNADE A row of columns and their entablatures, as in a covered walkway.

CONSOLE A large, ornamental bracket, usually of a scroll shape, most often used in cornices and at doors or windows. A *modillion* is small by comparison.

COQUINA A distinctive Southern coastal building stone showing the varied shells that comprise it.

CORBEL A projecting piece sup-porting a beam.

CORINTHIAN ORDER One of the three basic classical column, capital, and entablature compositions; it has a molded base, fluted shaft, and capital with scrolled acanthus leaf ornament (see also *Doric* and *Ionic*).

CORNER PILASTER A pilaster at the corner of a building, one or more storeys in height.

CORNER WINDOW One or more windows on each face of the corner of a building, much used in the Prairie and Modern styles.

CORNICE The projecting finish at the top of a building or porch, be-tween the eaves and the wall, usu-ally decorated with moldings, den-tils and/or modillions; in the classi-cal orders, it is the top piece of the entablature.

COVE A large concave molding, usually found in a cornice.

CRESTING Decorative cast-iron or terra-cotta ornament along the roof ridge of a building.

CROCKET A projecting, shaped ornament used in Gothic Revival buildings on spires or pinnacles.

CROSS GABLE A gable placed at right angles to the main gable of a building, most often facing the front.

CUPOLA A small, usually domed turret with windows on top of a roof.

DENTIL One of the small, closely spaced blocks in a cornice; modil-lions are larger and shaped.

DOOR HEAD The top piece or archi-trave of a door frame, often molded and decorated.

DORIC ORDER One of the three basic classic column, capital, and entablature compositions; it has no base, a fluted shaft, and a simple molded capital below the entabla-ture. The principal variation is the Tuscan, which has a plain, unfluted column with a base.

DOUBLE-HUNG WINDOW A win-dow comprised of two sashes, slid-ing vertically with or without pul-leys or weights.

DOUBLE PILE Two rooms deep (as in a double-pile house).

DRESSED RUBBLE Natural field stone, partially evened and smoothed. Unfinished stone is called rubble stone.

EAVES The edges of a roof which project over the wall of the build-ing.

ENTABLATURE In the classical orders, the arrangement of moldings and ornament in the horizontal member joining the tops of column capitals and comprising, from top to bottom, cornice, frieze, and archi-trave.

EYEBROW DORMER A low, wide, sometimes curved-headed dormer window.

FACADE A face or elevation of a building, as in front facade, meaning the front face of a house.

FACHWERK German term for tradi-tional Germanic half-timbering construction with a masonry infill.

FANLIGHT An arched transom over a door, usually with radial muntins.

FASCIA A horizontal cover board or, in classical architecture, part of the entablature architrave.

FIVE-PART PLAN Also known as a *Palladian plan*, the English and Amer-ican mansion form comprised of a main block with, on each side, hyphens (narrow wings), which connect to terminal flanking buildings or pavilions, sometimes called *flankers*.

FLEMISH BOND Brick bond with alternating headers and stretchers, common in the 18th and late-19th centuries. The headers used often have a black glaze for visual effect (glazed headers).

FLUSH SIDING Smooth wood siding that does not lap over the previous board (as clapboards do); also known as matched siding.

FRIEZE In classical architecture, one of the principal parts of the entablature above the column, usually flat, sometimes decorated; it lies between the cornice and the architrave.

FRIEZE WINDOW Small horizontal or oval window set into the frieze of a building.

FRONTISPIECE Decorative composition enriching a doorway; it may include columns or pilasters, consoles, cornice, or pediment.

GABLE The triangular portion of an end wall between the roof slopes and under the roof ridge.

GAMBREL A roof form with two pitches to the roof, the lower one steeper than the one above.

HACIENDA Spanish term for a self-sufficient rural estate or farm; by extension, a house.

HALF-TIMBERED A heavy wood-braced frame filled in with brick, stone, or wattle-and-daub (sticks and clay); also called *fachwerk*.

HALL-AND-PARLOR PLAN A basic early house plan with two rooms side by side.

HEADER In brickwork, the small end face of the brick.

HIP ROOF A gable roof sloping inward on all four sides.

HOOD MOLD, OR LABEL Decorative molding above a window or door that continues part way down the sides.

HYPHEN Small connecting wing or passage between the main block of a house and a wing.

I-HOUSE A vernacular house one room deep, two storeys high, and three or five bays wide, forming an I-shape.

INGLENOOK A seated recess at the side of a large fireplace and, by extension, any seated recessed area.

IONIC ORDER One of the three basic classical column, capital, and entablature compositions; it has a base, fluted columns, and a capital with a cushioned, scrolled volute below the entablature.

JERKIN HEAD A gable roof with the ends partially clipped at an angle.

JETTY OR OVERHANG A projecting, oversailing upper part of a building, common in 17th-century New England.

JIB DOOR A door formed from a window, in which the panel under the window opens as a half door when the sash is slid to its upper position.

LANCET, OR POINTED, ARCH The basic Gothic arch, with a pointed apex; its height is greater than its width. Variations include the *equilateral arch*, where the width is the same as the height, and the *dropped arch*, where the arch is wider than it is high.

MANSARD ROOF A traditional French roof design with the lower roof pitch almost vertical, creating a full attic storey, and with a low slope above. The attic slope may be straight, concave, or convex.

MODILLION A small decorative, shaped, blocklike ornament used in a series in a cornice.

MONITOR WINDOW A continuous small roof window usually extending across the entire building width.

MUNTINS Thin pieces of wood or steel used to hold the individual panes of glass in a window sash.

OCULUS A round opening or window at the top of a dome.

ORIEL A bay window that does not descend to the ground but is supported on corbels or brackets.

OVERMANTEL The panel above a fireplace mantel.

PALLADIAN WINDOW A featured window comprised of a large center window topped by a fanlight, with narrow windows flanking the principal one.

PARAPET A raised wall above a roofline.

PARTY WALL A common wall shared by two adjoining houses, each of which uses the wall structurally; hence, party-wall house or row house, and, today, a town house.

PATTERN BOOK An architectural book containing building designs.

PAVILION A wing or section of a building, or a small outbuilding.

PEDIMENT A triangular face of a roof gable, often topping a line of columns on a building, or a similar small form above a door or window. The inside space is the *tympanum*. Broken pediments are not completed either at the top or along the bed.

PENDANTS In Gothic Revival architecture, a decorative form hanging from above, as on the eaves or from an ornamental plaster ceiling.

PENT EAVE A small, rooflike projection along the wall of a house, usually between floors; common in colonial architecture.

PIANO NOBILE The principal storey of a house, raised above grade.

PIAZZA A covered gallery or verandah, or in 18th-century row houses, the narrow wing between the front and rear blocks of the house, usually with a door to the yard.

PIER An upright masonry structure, usually square, supporting an upper floor or roof.

PILASTER A shallow column built against the wall of a building.

PORTE COCHÈRE A covered, open-sided structure for vehicles adjoining a house on the front or side.

PORTICO A featured entrance porch, usually in the form of the pedimented, columned portico of classical architecture. If the pedimented portico projects from the building it is *prostyle*; if it recedes, it is *in antes*. If there are four columns it is *tetrastyle*; six, *hexastyle*; eight, *octastyle*, to cite the most common types. Thus a building may have, for example, a *tetrastyle prostyle* portico.

QUATREFOIL In Gothic architecture, a four-lobed or cusped decorative figure formed within a circle; if there are three lobes, it is *trefoil*, etc.

RIDGE The peak of a gable roof.

SASH A frame for glass in a window or door. Double-hung sash windows have two sashes, for example, while casements have one or more. If a window is fixed, it is considered one sash.

SASH DOOR A door with a window or, if fully glazed, sometimes called a French door.

SCROLLWORK Decorative Victorian saw-cut ornament.

SHED ROOF A roof with a single slope.

SHOTGUN HOUSE A narrow, deep house, one room wide, usually one storey high. A second storey at the rear makes it a *camelback shotgun*.

SIDELIGHTS Narrow fixed sash (lights) flanking a door, sometimes with fancy ornamental muntins.

SPINDLE WORK Decorative Victorian turned woodwork.

STOOP A platform at an entrance to a house, smaller than a porch.

STUCCO Waterproof plaster for exterior walls, often with a finish of small pebbles (*pebbledash*).

TABBY Early American form of mass concrete, using oyster shells.

TRANSOM Glazed sash over an interior or exterior door or exterior; sometimes operating, sometimes fixed.

TYMPANUM The triangular space enclosed by a pediment.

VERANDAH Typically, a large porch extending around two or more sides of a house.

WATER TABLE A projecting base course, usually extending to the first-floor level.

WEATHERBOARDS, OR CLAPBOARDS Board covering for exterior walls, in which each course of boards partially overlaps the one below it.

WINDER STAIR A three-run or circular stair turning on itself, typically placed in a corner. Used separately, the term *winder* refers to the angled corner tread of such a stair.

INDEX